READER'S DIGEST

EXTREME
NATURE

EXTREME LIFE

Nature tests out extreme designs in every branch of the living world. The result is an incredibly varied array of living things, ranging from birds smaller than bumblebees to trees that keep growing for up to 5000 years.

▼ **BIGGEST SINGLE FLOWER**
Measuring up to 1 m across, the bowl-shaped flower of *Rafflesia arnoldii* is the world's largest individual bloom. Its overpowering odour of rotting meat attracts flies that pollinate it.

◄ **HEAVIEST INSECT**
Male goliath beetles, from tropical Africa, can weigh up to 100 g – that is about three times the weight of the average mouse. These huge insects feed on sap and fruit, and they fly after dark, making a sound like a distant motorbike as they steer between the trees.

▶ **GREATEST GNAWER**
Using their spectacularly powerful teeth as cutting tools, beavers gnaw through trees to build their dams. These can be hundreds of metres long, and they are constantly patched up and repaired by their owners to ensure that they remain watertight. Handed on down the generations, large dams can remain in place for over a century. The longest beaver dam ever measured was in Montana, USA, and was 700 m long.

▼ **SMALLEST FLOWERING PLANT**
Wolffia plants look like specks of
green dust scattered across the
surface of ditches and ponds.
Each plant can be as little
as 0.3 mm across, and
their flowers are so small
that they are invisible to
the naked eye.

▼ **BIGGEST BUTTERFLY**
The female Queen Alexandra's
birdwing has a wingspan of
up to 28 cm. One of the
rarest butterflies, it lives
in the forests of Papua
New Guinea, and lays
its eggs on climbing
plants that reach
high up into the
treetops.

▼ **SMALLEST SNAKE**
The lesser Antillean threadsnake
grows to a maximum length of about
12 cm. Like other threadsnakes, it has
a cylindrical worm-like body, and no
teeth in its upper jaw.

EXTREME PERFORMANCE

• FASTEST HEARTBEAT
Hummingbirds and small bats have
the fastest heartbeats of all animals.
In flight, the hearts of both can beat
1200 times a minute.

**• HIGHEST BODY
TEMPERATURE**
Small songbirds have an average
body temperature of about 41°C,
which is the highest of any warm-
blooded animal.

• LONGEST BREATH-HOLDING
Southern elephant seals can hold
their breath for over two hours – the
longest time for any diving mammal.

• SLOWEST BREATHING
Cruising at the surface, a sperm
whale breathes between one and
three times a minute – the slowest
rate for any active animal.

• SURVIVING DROUGHT
Microscopic animals called
tardigrades can lose 99 per cent
of their body water and still survive.
Human cells die after losing
12 per cent.

• SURVIVING COLD
Some animals can survive being
frozen solid. They include insects
that breed in Arctic pools and some
kinds of frog.

• HIBERNATING
On the fringes of the Arctic, some
species of ground squirrel hibernate
for up to nine months a year.

• REPRODUCING
Many single-celled creatures –
including amoebas – are potentially
immortal. When they are mature,
they reproduce by dividing in two.

• FASTING
Large snakes may eat less than once
a month, but many spiders can live
for over a year without eating.

• FEASTING
With their large, loosely hinged
mouths, deep-sea gulper eels can eat
fish bigger than themselves, an
adaptation for life in a habitat where
food is hard to find.

• EXCRETING
Aphids feed on sugars that are
dissolved in sap. To get enough food,
they often have to get rid of up to
ten times their own body weight of
water a day.

• PROCESSING FOOD
Because it has such a high metabolic
rate, a shrew uses up food over 100
times faster than an elephant.

MANY LIVING THINGS UNUSUAL TACTICS AND TO CATCH PREY, OUTWIT THEIR ENVIRONMENT. STRENGTH, SPEED OR OTHERS, SUCCESS SLOW OR SMALL, ON STRIKING OUT. IN THE NATURE PUSHES LIFE

HAVE DEVELOPED VERY SKILLS IN THEIR BID ENEMIES AND ADAPT TO FOR SOME, SUPREME SIZE IS KEY. FOR DEPENDS ON BEING BLENDING IN OR BATTLE FOR SURVIVAL, TO ITS EXTREMES.

◄ SMALLEST ANIMAL
The world's smallest animals are rotifers – tiny transparent creatures that live in freshwater all over the planet. Some measure just 0.04 mm, which means they are dwarfed by many bacteria.

◄ LONGEST INSECT
With its legs stretched out, the tropical stick insect *Pharnacia kirbyi* measures up to 50 cm long. Despite its extraordinary size, it moves very slowly, and may spend its entire life on a single tree.

▼ SMALLEST FROG
Many of the world's smallest frogs live in Central America and the islands of the Caribbean. The record for the smallest is held by *Smithillus limbatus*, a species from Cuba. An adult can be as little as 1.2 cm long.

► SMALLEST VERTEBRATE
Discovered in 2006, a tiny tropical fish called *Paedocypris progenetica* is the smallest animal with a backbone. It lives in swampy pools on the island of Sumatra, and even fully grown is just 8 mm long.

▲ LONGEST-LIVED INDIVIDUAL PLANT
Bristlecone pines are the world's oldest living things, with a lifespan of up to 5000 years. These trees grow high up in the mountains of the American West, where cold temperatures slow their growth.

◀ HIGHEST-LIVING MAMMAL
The yak lives at altitudes of up to 6000 m in the Himalayas. Yaks are kept warm by a coat of dense shaggy hair, which in winter can reach down to the ground.

▶ SMALLEST BIRD
With a body measuring just 5 cm, the bee hummingbird from Cuba is smaller than many insects. It weighs around 1.8 g and lays the smallest egg of any bird – about the size of a pea – in a nest the size of an egg cup.

18 **19** **20** **21** **22** **23** **24** **25** **26**

46 47 48 49 50 51 52 53 54 55 56 57 58 59 60 61 62 63 64 65 66

▼ SMALLEST LAND MAMMAL
The pygmy white-toothed shrew measures as little as 6 cm from its nose to the tip of its tail, making it the world's smallest terrestrial mammal. Unlike mice, shrews are carnivorous. Because they are so small, they have to hunt and eat around the clock to avoid starving to death.

▼ LONGEST CENTIPEDE
Found in tropical South America, the giant centipede *Scolopendra morsitans* can be up to 33 cm long. This venomous nocturnal predator feeds on lizards, frogs and roosting birds, attacking them with its poison claws.

EXTREME
NATURE

1 WHEN SPEED COUNTS

2 TESTS OF STRENGTH

5 BRIGHTEST AND BEST

6 HIDDEN POWERS

3 MIGHT IS RIGHT

4 SMALL IS BEAUTIFUL

7 OUTWITTING THE ENEMY

INTRODUCTION

HUMANS HAVE ALWAYS BEEN FASCINATED BY THE UNUSUAL IN NATURE. Myths and folklore abound with weird creatures and plants with extraordinary powers, but in nature fact can be far more astonishing than fiction. From the icy poles to the steamy jungle, from the desert to the deep seabed, living things can be found that have evolved extreme characteristics to enable them to survive in a particular niche or a hostile environment.

In November 1861, the crew of the French steamship *Alecton* came face to face with a dramatic example of this phenomenon. Near the Canary Islands, the lookout spotted a giant squid floating at the sea's surface. This was the first time that anyone had seen one of these **colossal animals** alive. Since that encounter, technology has come on by leaps and bounds. Radio tracking has revealed some of the **epic journeys** made by birds, and remarkable experiments are helping to unravel the mystery of how they navigate. Special recording equipment enables scientists to study the **infrasound calls** of elephants and whales, while high-speed cameras reveal what happens when a flea makes a **gravity-defying jump**, or when a cheetah breaks into a **record-breaking sprint**. Thanks to satellite communications and the internet,

scientists can also gather data from the most remote places on Earth, such as the sea's depths or polar ice. Biologists can monitor the heartbeat of sperm whales or elephant seals during their **incredible dives**, or the body temperature of male emperor penguins as they incubate their eggs through the Antarctic winter. Remote-controlled cameras can observe female polar bears in their dens, or the **world's biggest columns** of marauding army ants as they make their way across the rainforest floor.

Extreme nature also involves many things that are invisible to the naked eye. Some microscopic animals can **survive for decades** without water or food, while **microscopic plants** provide the food that fuels almost all of animal life at sea. Further still down the ladder of scale, bacteria are even tougher and live in every habitat on Earth. They existed long before animals and plants and some of them – aptly called **extremophiles** – are so resilient they could even survive in space.

No one can predict what the future holds for planet Earth, or what it will look like in a million years from now, but one thing is certain: living things of some sort will still be going to extremes in order to survive, just as they have done since life first emerged.

WHEN SP
COUNTS

EED

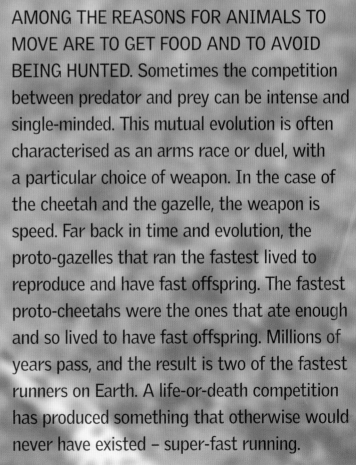

AMONG THE REASONS FOR ANIMALS TO MOVE ARE TO GET FOOD AND TO AVOID BEING HUNTED. Sometimes the competition between predator and prey can be intense and single-minded. This mutual evolution is often characterised as an arms race or duel, with a particular choice of weapon. In the case of the cheetah and the gazelle, the weapon is speed. Far back in time and evolution, the proto-gazelles that ran the fastest lived to reproduce and have fast offspring. The fastest proto-cheetahs were the ones that ate enough and so lived to have fast offspring. Millions of years pass, and the result is two of the fastest runners on Earth. A life-or-death competition has produced something that otherwise would never have existed – super-fast running.

EXTREME PERFORMANCE

ONE SECOND A CHEETAH CAN BE PERFECTLY STILL, PERHAPS CROUCHED AT THE END OF A LONG STALKING PROCESS. Then it explodes into speed, and three seconds later it can be travelling at more than 80 km/h. If you floored the accelerator on the average new car, it would take you at least twice that long to go that fast, and the cheetah usually keeps accelerating after it reaches the 80 km mark. The absolute speed record for a land animal is held by a cheetah in Kenya, clocked at 103 km/h.

Every second counts

A cheetah's exertion is as short as it is sudden. If it hasn't caught what it is after in less than a minute and over a distance of less than 300 m, it becomes out of breath and has to stop. It pants and can hardly move at all for at least 20 minutes. Its body temperature has risen, according to some estimates, to 40°C. Like any exhausted animal, it needs to recover the oxygen that has been lost from its muscle fibres, but it also needs to expel a huge build-up of carbon dioxide. Then there is the matter of the lactic acid that those highly specialised, 'fast' muscle fibres produce in quantity – excessive lactic acid is a famous cause of fatigue. The brain has overheated along with the rest of the body and has to be cooled by the air the cheetah blows through its sinuses and across its wet tongue.

But all that is just immediate recuperation and happens whether the cheetah has caught its prey or not. The really serious loss, if the chase has failed, is the stuff of life – food, or energy. A cheetah cannot store energy: it has very little fat on its body. Four or five consecutive chases with no result and the cheetah will probably die.

So a cheetah's life is almost entirely dependent on outrunning other animals. And not just any other animals: because a cheetah is lightweight, it has to go for lightweight animals, and these, like cheetahs themselves, tend to be fast. A Thompson's gazelle, one of the cheetah's main targets, has been timed doing a speed of 94.2 km/h. Not only does a cheetah have to be faster than that, but in every contest the gazelle gets about a 50 m head start.

SPECIALISED BODY The long spine works as a spring for the powerful back legs to give the cheetah added reach for each step.

RACING MACHINE Besides gazelles, cheetahs use their sprinting speed against springboks, duikers, steenboks, young warthogs, hares and occasionally larger antelopes, such as wildebeest, kudu, hartebeest, oryx, roans and sables. They have also been known to catch birds.

Built for speed

The cheetah is the only cat that cannot retract its claws. They are permanently extended and give traction in the same way that spiked football shoes do. For aerodynamics, the cheetah has a small head, and for balance very narrow shoulders and hips and a long tail that, when the animal is virtually flying, acts as a rudder, much as a bird's tail does. A cheetah's instant start and its ability to turn quickly and to leap are made possible by a long, flexible, almost rubbery spine. The long tendons in a cheetah's legs also act as elastic springs.

Cheetahs run with what is known as a rotary gallop, which is to say the footwork describes a circle: left hind leg, right hind, right fore, left fore. This differs from a horse, for example, which has a transverse gallop: left hind, right hind, left fore, right fore. While the transverse gallop is steadier and best for good speed over long distances, the rotary gallop – which

gazelles also use – is faster over the short stretch and best for sudden changes of direction. Also, although a cheetah (with a height and body length of about 80 cm) is much smaller than a horse, the two animals have the same maximum stride length of 7 m. At top speed a cheetah can hit 3.5 strides a second compared to a horse's 2.25. And a cheetah is one of the very few animals that, when running, can have phases when all four feet are off the ground.

An adult cheetah can outrun anything that has a mind to chase it, but what it cannot do very well is defend a fresh kill from encroaching lions or hyenas. And since these two predators tend to take special notice of a cheetah making a kill, and since a cheetah can't afford to have too many kills stolen, the best it can usually do is bolt the food down while it can. A cheetah is the world's fastest runner all right, but it also has to be one of the fastest eaters.

THE LONG RUN

LEAP OF FAITH A springbok leaps up in the air, hanging in space and seeming to defy gravity.

THE SPRINGBOK IS CAPABLE OF REMARKABLE BOUTS OF HIGH-JUMPING KNOWN AS PRONKING. It can also come close to a gazelle for speed – up to 88 km/h according to some reports. From a standing position, this dainty little antelope from the drier parts of southern and southwestern Africa moves its feet close together, stiffens its legs, curves its body, lowers its head and shoots straight up in the air, sometimes as high as 2 m. And when it comes down, either on the same spot or a bit ahead of where it was before, it will often jump right back up again – repeating the action five to six times in rapid succession, like a bouncing ball. While the springbok does this, a pouch on its lower back opens, revealing a crest of long, erect, white hairs, which are taken to be a signal to the rest of the herd.

High-jumpers

A few other antelopes and gazelles indulge in pronking, but none do it as high, as frequently or as characteristically as a springbok. The exact cause of this behaviour is unknown. Some biologists see it mainly as an expression of excitement or as a sexual display. But it could be both of those things and also an anti-predator strategy.

predators – black-backed jackals seem to have the most success hunting them – because in a herd that large a few are bound to be unlucky. The kind of fatalism that surrounds that fact is what persuades prey animals to seek the relative, but never absolute, safety of numbers. And it seems that their impressive bouts of leaping help to make a long-shot longer.

The big trek

Before Europeans settled in South Africa, springboks would suddenly and spontaneously go on what the early settlers called a 'trekbokke'. There was nothing seasonal about this, and no one has ever been able to determine what would spark it off. It

Springboks have plenty of predators: as well as cheetahs, there are lions, hyenas, wild dogs and jackals. The antelope could be pronking to get high enough to spot any of these coming, either in the distance or in tall grass. Once a predator is spotted, the pronking seems to increase – each springbok bounces more, and more individuals start bouncing. At this point the function of the pronking appears to change – to alert the rest of the herd, which can number in the hundreds, and to confuse or distract the predator. It could also be intimidation: a way of saying, I'm super-fit, and you'd be wasting your energy trying to catch me.

The finale comes when the hundreds of springboks suddenly stop pronking and scatter in all directions, taking leaps that are longer than their jumps are high. Of course, springboks do get caught by

The springbok moves its feet close together, stiffens its legs, curves its body, lowers its head and shoots straight up in the air. And when it comes down it will often jump right back up again, repeating the action five or six times, like a bouncing ball.

would happen in the Karoo, South Africa's central plains area. All the springbok herds, which numbered in their hundreds to begin with, would start moving towards the same place, until they all converged in a massive herd of hundreds of thousands. Along the way, virtually every blade of grass and leaf of tree would be eaten. As human settlers began to pour in, tolerance of springboks diminished. Finally, so many of them were slaughtered and so much of the Karoo was fenced in that the trekbokke stopped happening, and only a fraction of the original springbok population has survived.

HARES

PRACTICALLY EVERYTHING THAT EATS MEAT EATS RABBITS AND HARES. According to one conservation report, 90 per cent of European and American lagomorphs, as the two animals are called, are eaten by predators. In fact, the main distinction between rabbits and hares is their different strategies for avoiding death. Rabbits go for thick cover, while hares get out in the open and run.

Their different survival strategies have, over millions of years, determined their preferred habitats – rabbits in forests, hares in fields – and even shaped their bodies. Rabbits are slow and compact with short legs, while hares are bigger – an adult weighs between 3 to 5 kg – more conspicuous and long-legged. Hares are also very fast. There is one report of a European brown hare (*Lepus europaeus*) travelling at 80 km/h, although the usual figure given for this hare's top speed is 72 km/h. Even the lower figure beats the world record for a racing greyhound (67 km/h) or a sprinting racehorse (69 km/h).

RACING HARES A pair of European brown hares chase across fields in Norfolk, England. No other British mammal is better able to survive in totally open habitats.

Catch me if you can

While greyhounds and thoroughbred sprinters do not have to keep up their speed for very long, hares – as hunters will testify – can keep going for almost an hour. A hare isn't just fast, either – it's evasive, outwitting pursuers with lots of jinks, sudden changes of direction, zig-zagging and even backtracking. What helps it greatly is the fact that it knows its territory. It has already scouted the possible courses it could take and can speed along them with the confidence that it won't have any collisions. There is a limit, though, to the amount of territory it can memorise, and anything chasing a hare will find itself running back and forth and in circles.

Enemy overhead

But if hares are so hard to catch, why do they have such high mortality? For one thing, their predators include medium to large birds of prey, such as owls and buzzards, and almost any animal that flies is faster and has a better view than an animal running along the ground. For another, the bulk of the mortality rate is suffered by the babies, or leverets, which are often left undefended. A hare doesn't lose quite so many young as a rabbit: it has been estimated that the average European rabbit loses around 30 offspring a year. It is the endeavour to replace such losses that gives them their main reputation – as one of the world's fastest-breeding mammals.

NO OTHER ANIMAL RUNS AS FAST

OVER LONG DISTANCES AS THE NORTH AMERICAN PRONGHORN.
The only surviving member of a prehistoric family, the deer-like pronghorn is unique on the planet. Relative to its size, it has a larger heart, windpipe and pair of lungs than any other mammal. Its blood is so rich in haemoglobin that it carries oxygen from lungs to muscles in greater quantity and quicker than any other mammal's blood. The muscles that benefit most from this are the lower-torso ones, which operate extremely light-boned legs. In its full 8 m stride, its forelegs push as far forward as they can go, and then the hind legs as far back, and when both meet right under the body, the body is, for that instant, entirely in the air. The upshot of this extreme physiology is an animal with a top speed of 88 km/h. That is almost as fast as a cheetah, but a pronghorn can keep going for much longer – the 88 km/h was recorded over a distance of 800 m, compared to a cheetah's usual 300 m. Pronghorns have been clocked at a steady 70 km/h over a distance of 6.4 km.

But why does a pronghorn need to run so fast and over such daunting distances? Certainly no North American predator – wolf, coyote or puma – can begin to keep up with it. The prevailing theory is that the pronghorn, as an ancient animal, could well be the survivor in an evolutionary struggle with an extinct American cheetah – a super-cheetah that could do high speeds at distances that today's African cheetah could only dream of attaining.

CLASS: Mammalia
ORDER: Artiodactyla
SPECIES: *Antilocapra americana*
HABITAT: Prairies
DISTRIBUTION: North America
KEY FEATURES: The fastest land animal over distance; its protruding eyes give it a 360° field of vision.

PRONGHORN

ROCKETING DOWN TO CATCH ITS PREY, NO OTHER CREATURE ON EARTH CAN MOVE AS FAST AS A PEREGRINE FALCON. The extent of this bird of prey's immense speed first became apparent in 1938 when an American pilot – after pulling out of a 273 km/h nose-dive – reported having been passed by a plunging peregrine 'as though the plane was standing still'. A peregrine in a dive, or stoop, of 1250 m could in theory reach a speed of 385 km/h. No one has actually clocked the bird at this top possible rate but a sky-diver has filmed one at 322 km/h.

Dive-bomber

A peregrine stooping is not really flying – it's coming out of the sky like a 1 kg feathered rock. These falcons get higher than most before they dive, so they reach higher speeds. Presumably they need the altitude and the resulting speed because their prey itself is so fast. Pigeons, for example, a staple peregrine food, can have a cruising speed of about 50 km/h and bursts of about 100 km/h, which is near the top speed for a cheetah. Peregrines also take domestic racing pigeons and some of those have been recorded at more than 160 km/h.

Record-breakers

Even racing pigeons don't get close to the speed records of wild birds, in flight rather than free-fall. There have been several contradictory claims for the fastest flyers, but the one that's most often repeated is for spinetail swifts, also

AERIAL ATTACK

known as Indian needletail swifts. In 1955 an observer with a stopwatch timed the flight of these birds as they crossed a 3.2 km-wide valley in Assam and reported them zipping over at a groundspeed of 323 km/h (see pages 26-7).

The aerial record for the best non-stop time over the longest distance is usually claimed for the wandering albatross, with a steady cruising windspeed of 56 km/h for 800 km. But a new record for verified non-stop distance alone was set in March 2007 by a satellite-tracked bar-tailed godwit, dubbed E-7 by scientists tracking its progress. Whether this is also some kind of speed record may have to wait for further calculation, but in less than two weeks this small bird, which was part of a flock on migration from New Zealand to Alaska, travelled from New Zealand's South Island, flew up between Queensland and New Caledonia, passed east of New Guinea and west of Guam, flew over the

STOOPS TO CONQUER With wings folded, a peregrine falcon makes a spectacular dive to catch its prey.

Yellow Sea and finally came to rest in North Korea. The bird had covered a staggering distance of 10 205 km, without eating, drinking, sleeping or taking any other pit stops. There are longer migrations than the godwit's: the most famous is probably the Arctic tern's – Arctic to Antarctic and back – but it is not known where, how often or even if the terns stop along the way.

The sky's the limit

The point about speed, distance and travel by air, as opposed to land or water, is that air is by far the easiest and smoothest medium for an animal to negotiate. Land animals are in a perpetual battle against gravity, constantly pushing off against the ground and being instantly pulled back to it. Travel by water is a little easier, in that the water supports an animal's weight, but it also puts up an enormous resistance to forward movement, usually dealt with by streamlining. While air animals also use stremlining, they rely to an even greater degree on lightness, which they have taken to its extreme. Once they can spread their wings and support themselves on air, there's not much barrier to going as fast as is feasible.

Into the arc

The irony is that the fastest bird of all – the peregrine – actually uses gravity to reach its amazing speed. It flies up high and then falls. Perhaps the real question is why doesn't it crash? It hurtles down at a speed never attained by any other animal, hits another speeding bird not far from the ground, then it opens its wings and immediately pulls out of the dive. Why doesn't it black out or smash into its intended prey and turn both birds into a pile of feathers? A recent discovery has shown that because of a quirk in the peregrine's eyesight and the need to keep its aim on the target, in the very last stages of the stoop the bird is not going at its previous 30°-45° angle, but comes in at an arc. The sheer speed makes it hard for an observer to notice this, but the falcon is pulling out of the dive and into flight before it reaches its prey. And this implies that the peregrine has been taking that last manoeuvre into account from the beginning of the stoop.

CATCH THE PIGEON A peregrine swoops on its quarry. It will use its speed to knock the bird out of the sky.

ASSISTED FLIGHT

WHEN A MAN WITH A STOPWATCH TIMES THE FLIGHT OF SPINETAIL SWIFTS he assumes they really are flying at the speed recorded on his watch, making them the world's fastest flyers. But are they? The truth is, the figures record the birds' groundspeed – that is, their speed as perceived relative to the ground. The stopwatch does not record what the air itself is doing. It doesn't say how much of the flight was done by the birds and how much by the wind; nor does it subtract the wind speed to record the birds' actual airspeed.

In fact, spinetail swifts have a habit of flying along the edges of weather fronts and in the turbulent air around thunderstorms. They are air animals, and they know how to use the air for assistance. So when their groundspeed was recorded as 323 km/h and they were declared to be the world's fastest flyers, this appears to have been wrong by about 200 km/h, because a spinetail swift's airspeed has subsequently been measured at 125 km/h.

To live and navigate in the air takes special adaptations, not least of which is lightness. Almost every part of a bird is built to minimise weight, and though its blood and muscle fibres operate with some very clever, weight-saving chemistry, there's still a lightness-imposed limit as to how much muscle a bird can have, and how strong it can be. But because the bird is light, and because the air moves with the ease it does, flying does not require that much muscle if the bird knows how to ride the wind. And birds do. They're sailors.

Riding the wind

Wind-assistance is mainly for long-haul flight. This can mean a daily flight across the countryside to feed, or the slow circling of a bird of prey – anything high and sustained. And the highest, most sustained and most dependent on the wind is

STAYING TOGETHER Canada geese fly in formation over Wisconsin. Birds take turns to lead the flock, rotating back into formation when they tire.

THE GLOBETROTTER The wandering albatross spends most of its life in flight. They commonly follow fishing boats, sometimes for days on end.

long-haul migration. At higher altitude, there's less air resistance, and the wind is steadier and more dependable. Migrating birds tend not to come down if they can help it – as a rule they want to get where they're going and don't appear to like pit stops.

Among the best-studied migrating birds are Canada geese, most of the eastern population of which breed around Hudson Bay and spend the winter in the southeastern USA. In everyday flight, they have an airspeed of about 65 km/h at an altitude of between 30 and 300 m. When they set off to go south, they rise to about 2800 m, where the thin air and the wind increase their groundspeed to 115 km/h and allow them to make the entire journey in about 20 hours. Going north in the spring they make a totally different journey. They want to reach their breeding ground when the temperature is right, and so as spring creeps up North America, the geese dawdle along behind. The line of temperature that they follow – known as an isotherm – is 16°C. They don't want to overshoot that. So they fly low and slow, and tend to spend the nights on the ground.

In formation

It has long been suspected that flocks fly in a 'V' formation to save energy, but only recently has it been proven. A French team making a feature film trained white pelicans to fly behind a plane. They monitored the birds' heart-rates, discovering that

these were lower when they flew together than when they flew solo. It seemed that when the pelicans all flapped their wings at the same time, they benefited from each other's airstream and were all able to glide more often. So birds can even ride the wind created by other birds.

Easy glider

The most famous wind-rider of them all is the wandering albatross. It is the largest of all the albatrosses and has the widest wingspan of any bird, typically around 3.5 m. It spreads its huge wings and soars over the Southern Ocean, snatching fish as it passes by. The wandering albatross can spend months in the air without ever touching land, sometimes being carried by the wind quite literally right round the world.

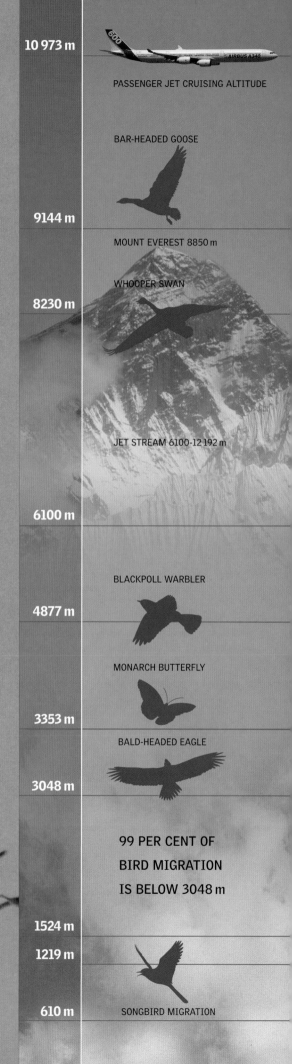

10 973 m
PASSENGER JET CRUISING ALTITUDE

BAR-HEADED GOOSE

9144 m

MOUNT EVEREST 8850 m

WHOOPER SWAN

8230 m

JET STREAM 6100-12 192 m

6100 m

BLACKPOLL WARBLER

4877 m

MONARCH BUTTERFLY

3353 m

BALD-HEADED EAGLE

3048 m

99 PER CENT OF BIRD MIGRATION IS BELOW 3048 m

1524 m

1219 m

SONGBIRD MIGRATION

610 m

RECORD-BREAKING INSECTS

COULD AN INSECT POSSIBLY REACH A SPEED OF 1287 KM/H? That's four football fields per second. Fast enough to create a sonic boom. That was the time claimed in 1927 for the deer botfly. In fact, the figure was wildly extravagant. To get the energy for such exertion the botfly would have to eat its own weight every second – but would not be able to because its head would have disintegrated with the stress of the speed. The example helps to illuminate the first sentence of a scientific paper published in 2003: 'The speed attainable by insects is currently poorly understood.' In this paper the two fastest flying insects are given as desert locusts and corn earworm moths, with average speeds of 33 and 28 km/h, respectively. It adds that 'many insects surely fly faster, but their airspeeds have yet to be studied with modern methods'.

FAST FOOD A scarlet darter dragonfly catches a damselfly. As its name suggests, the darter attacks its prey suddenly and rapidly.

The forward sweep of the wings – modelled on those of a fruitfly – is at an angle so steep it would cause a bird or a plane to crash, but on the scale of an insect gives lift.

HOVERING ABOUT A striped hawkmoth uses its very long tongue to gather nectar from night-flowering plants. Hawkmoths are the only moths that can hover.

Other, less cautious sources agree that the fastest insects can be found among the various dragonflies, with 'verified' speeds of between 30 and 60 km/h. And probably the fastest flying insect ever – if size is anything to go by – was the extinct *Meganeura monyi* dragonfly, which lived in the Permian period, more than 250 million years ago. Its wingspan was as much as 75 cm, compared to the 19 cm of Australia's southern giant darner dragonfly, the largest one living today.

Speed trials

Difficult as it is to separate the airspeed from the groundspeed of birds, it's yet more difficult to do the same for insects, since any little ripple of breeze qualifies as a blast to something so light. Scientists have tried all sorts of tricks to get around this problem. They've timed insects with stopwatches to get average speeds, put them in wind tunnels or cages, tethered them, used cameras, radar, remote sensing and computer modelling and, with a telescope, measured an insect's progress across a full moon. One man even claimed to have had horseflies chasing, and catching, plastic airgun pellets, with the result that one horsefly species, *Hybomitra hinei*, is the champion flyer at 145 km/h.

Other speeds of varying reliability include another horsefly, *Tabanus bovinus*, 45 km/h; an unknown species of bee, 56 km/h; the black cutworm moth, 113 km/h; the southern giant darner dragonfly, 97.2 km/h; the monarch butterfly, 40.3 km/h; and the striped hawkmoth, 40 km/h. The latter two are perhaps best known for their endurance. Their migrations take them on journeys of hundreds, even thousands, of miles, and they cover these distances in surprisingly fast times.

RUNNERS AND JUMPERS

Running speeds and jumping heights of insects are much easier to measure than their airspeeds.

Top three fastest runners

INSECT		SPEED (km/h)
	Australian tiger beetle (*Cicindela hudsoni*)	9
	Australian tiger beetle (*C. eburneola*)	6.7
	American cockroach	5.5

Top three highest jumpers

INSECT		HEIGHT (cm)
	Leafhopper	70
	Click beetle	30
	Cat flea	24

How do they fly?

The principles of flight that apply to birds – and, for that matter, to aeroplanes – do not apply to insects. How insect wings actually operate, down to the finest detail, has only recently been worked out by a University of California team. They have built a 'robofly', a Plexiglass-winged robotic insect that might some day have some military use and whose development is partly funded by the US Defense Advanced Research Projects Agency. Robofly is modelled on a fruit fly, and the wings don't just flap – they move up and down and back and forth, and they rotate. They use a mechanism called 'delayed stall', a forward sweep of the wings at an angle so steep it would cause a bird or a plane to crash, but on the scale of an insect gives lift. Then there's 'rotational circulation': the wings rotate backwards, creating backspin and providing even more lift. Still more comes from 'wake capture', whereby the wings shoot backwards to pluck energy from the wake of the immediately previous forward stroke.

Another study, looking at insect flight evolution, has suggested that unlike birds' wings – which probably evolved by way of forelegs with gliding membranes – insect wings may have developed from swimming mechanisms in their shrimp-like ancestors. Once some of these creatures left the sea, they were light enough to keep 'swimming' through the air. But not, fortunately, faster than the speed of sound: the 1287 km/h of the deer botfly has now been reliably corrected and established at 40 km/h.

FULL SAIL AHEAD The distinctive dorsal fin stretches almost the entire length of the sailfish's body.

RECORDS UNDER WATER

A SAILFISH ONCE UNREELED 91 M OF FISHING LINE IN THREE SECONDS – THAT'S 109 KM/H. It sounds like a fisherman's tale, but it happened during official, monitored trials. It wasn't all swimming – there was a lot of leaping involved – but it is generally agreed that sailfish are the sea's fastest movers. Its top speed does allow for some leaping, but mostly involves swimming through a medium 750 times denser than air and doing it faster than a cheetah runs.

What makes a sailfish so quick? For a start it's big – up to 100 kg in weight and 340 cm long – and, in water, size gives animals a speed advantage because swimming involves being wet. A layer of water sticks to the body of anything trying to

STRONG SWIMMER The fast-moving shortfin mako shark can leap clear of the water to heights of 6 m.

SPEED MATCH Equally fast as its prey, but far greater in size and strength, a killer whale catches a Dall's porpoise in Alaska, tossing it triumphantly in the air.

move through it, and the weight of that extra layer has to be pulled along with the body itself. Since small animals have more body surface relative to their size than large animals, the latter have relatively less wetness weighing them down.

Streamlining helps, too, because less water has to be pushed aside. The perfect streamlining is pretty much a sailfish's shape, tapered at both ends, with an elongated sword-like bill. For lift, the best fins are ones that are flattened on the lower surface and high and rounded on the upper. In the case of the sailfish, the upper fin is a little too high for the best streamlining when it's going very fast, so the fish lowers most of its large sail into a groove on its back, raising it occasionally to use as a rudder to make turns. The sail may also be raised when the sailfish feels threatened. For thrust, the sailfish has the perfect tail: a large crescent on a narrow stalk.

Muscle power

Muscles also play a vital role in speed. Swimming animals have two kinds, and they operate in different ways. Exactly how is complicated, but essentially they have white muscle for instant speed, and red muscle for some speed and lots of stamina. Most fish have mainly white muscle, so they can go fast in short bursts but tire easily. The fastest fish, including sailfish, swordfish, tuna and a few sharks, augment their white muscle with strips of red, which enables them to sustain their speed.

For red muscle to perform at top efficiency, it needs to be served by highly oxygenated warm blood. So fish with red

muscle – the fastest – are warm-blooded like marine mammals and unlike the vast majority of fish species. After sailfish, the next fastest fish are swordfish, at 97 km/h; marlin, 80; wahoo, 77; yellowfin tuna, 75; and bluefin tuna, 70. The speediest marine mammals are the killer whale and Dall's porpoise, both 55 km/h; the shortfin pilot whale, 49; and the largest animal in the world, the blue whale, which can reach 48 km/h.

Speeding sharks

Sharks are generally slower than bony fish because, over a very long evolutionary period hundreds of millions of years ago, they abandoned bones for cartilage in the interests of flexibility. To move fast in water, the best body is a stiff one, with as few vertebrae as possible in the backbone – a good description of a sailfish or marlin. However, not only does the shortfin mako shark have flexible cartilage instead of bone, it also has 180 cartilaginous vertebrae in its spine. And yet it can swim at 50 km/h, while two other fast sharks – the great white and the blue shark – can swim at speeds of 40 and 39 km/h, respectively. So how do these species do it?

The answer is that they, too, have red as well as white muscle and warm blood – making them, along with several other species of shark, the world's only warm-blooded, non-bony animals. Also, according to a recent discovery, these sharks have the ability to pressurise their thick skin and flex themselves until they are rigid. So sharks are a lot slower than sailfish, but way ahead of the fastest recorded time for a human swimmer – 8.11 km/h.

ESCAPING INTO THE AIR

FISH OUT OF WATER
The needlefish can be ten or more times longer than it is wide. Its ice pick-like beak is filled with teeth.

Needlefish first try to escape in swirling, silvery shoals. But as threats intensify, they simply get out of the water, shooting above and skimming along the surface for moments at a time.

THERE ARE CERTAIN FISH THAT CAN QUITE LITERALLY FLY THROUGH THE AIR TO ESCAPE PREDATORS. It is interesting to imagine what it must be like for the pursuer. Say you're a dolphin-fish, a tuna or a squid, and you're closing in on a fairly fast-swimming fish that's still well within your power to catch and hold, but just as you're about to do that, it disappears. While you're left looking around for it, and if the water's clear enough and you've got very good eyes – and if you're a squid, that's a possibility – it suddenly reappears 100 or more metres further on, as if it has gone into and out of another dimension. And from the point of view of an underwater animal, that's exactly what it has done.

Up, up and away

There are two types of flying fish – those with two wings and those with four. In the two-wing, only the pectoral fins (the ones where the arms would be if fish had arms) are enlarged and stiffened. Four-wing flying fish also have a pair of smaller pelvic fins, which act as stabilisers. In either case, the pursued fish, its wings folded in, swims at about 35 km/h towards the water's surface. It zooms into the air at a shallow angle, opens its wings and then gets further thrust by rapidly thrashing the water with the long lower lobe of its tail. When the fish is completely launched, it glides, without flapping, at about a metre above the water and at twice its top swimming speed for up to 200 m if it's a four-wing, and about half that if it's a two-wing.

There are nine genera of flying fish, ranging in size from 15 to 50 cm. All are found in seas where surface waters are above 20°C – in other words, the tropics. A high temperature is necessary because the fish are cold-blooded and at cooler temperatures wouldn't be able to muster the muscle-power to fly.

Needlefish

Needlefish are long, thin relatives of flying fish who also leave the water to keep from being eaten. They gather in huge numbers near the sea's surface in both tropical and temperate waters. There are many species of needlefish, and they are typically about 30 cm long, although some of the bigger ones can reach 90 cm.

Needlefish predators include dolphins and porpoises, cod and pollock, bluefish and similar fish, which they first try to escape in swirling, silvery, predator-confusing shoals. As the threats intensify, however, they get out of the water – rapidly undulating their long bodies. Masses of them can be seen shooting above and skimming along the surface for moments at a time. They are not as expert or coordinated as flying fish, and when they panic and are near land, they often beach themselves.

ON THE WING Flying fish use their remarkable aerial talent to escape predators. During take-off (right), the larger lobe of the tail acts like an outboard motor.

THERE ARE CERTAIN MOVEMENTS IN THE ANIMAL KINGDOM THAT ARE SO FAST THEY ARE INVISIBLE TO THE HUMAN EYE. The punch of a stomatopod – also known as a mantis shrimp – accelerates at a much faster speed than a rocket needs to escape the pull of the Earth.

HIGH-SPEED REACTIONS

The stomatopods are found in coastal waters all over the world, and they all hit, or stab, hard. There are thousands of species, which fall into two groups: smashers and spearers. The latter have forelimbs with spines that they use to spear soft-bodied animals, such as fish and shrimps. The smashers have clubs for crushing crabs, clams, snails and the like. A smasher can approach a crab – a creature much larger than itself – and proceed to break its claws, legs and carapace before dragging it back to its rocky burrow to eat it. A smaller creature, such as a clam or snail, will be dragged back whole and opened by smashing it against the burrow wall.

When scientists began to look more closely at the stomatopod's forelimbs, however, they realised that there wasn't enough muscle to produce anything near the force required for a blow moving at a speed of 20 m per second. In fact, the muscle was too weak by a factor of 100. What the stomatopod used instead appeared to be a catch-and-spring mechanism. The animal draws its forelimbs up, almost as if in a boxing pose, and a strong, saddle-shaped, elastic piece of chitin – normally the main

MIDGE PATROL In a swarm of midges, there is constant sexual competition among the males. Those that mate with the most females are the most aerobatic ones – the fastest and with the fastest wingbeat.

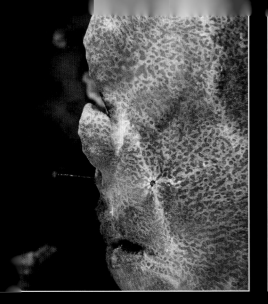

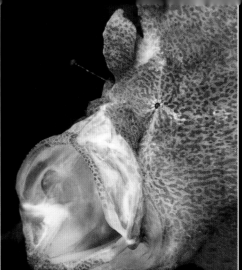

HOOVERING UP The frogfish wriggles its lure, then sucks up unsuspecting fish, opening and closing its mouth in 15 milliseconds.

Master of disguise

The frogfish is a vertebrate with high-speed reactions. It inhabits the Indian and Pacific oceans and is a master of camouflage. It can change its colour to match its often pebbly, shallow-seafloor background. It can look like a sponge or can grow appendages and warts to mimic seaweeds. The frogfish also has a dorsal fin that's become a sort of fishing rod, with an artificial lure dangling conveniently near its mouth. It can elbow up to a school of feeding fish, wriggle its lure and suck in the nearest fish – so fast that the other fish don't notice.

substance in insect exoskeletons – is squeezed and bent to hold the limb that way, locked into place. When the stomatopod is ready to strike, it uses its muscle to unlock its forelimb, and as the saddle suddenly straightens out, the club at the end is flung down on its prey.

Caught in a trap

The trap-jaw ant of Central and South America also uses the catch-and-spring mechanism when it closes its mandibles. Researchers have only recently discovered that after using muscles in its head to crank its mandibles open, the ant keeps them open with a pair of latches. When it finds its prey or is threatened by something, it releases the latches, and the jaws close at speeds of 35-64 m per second, up to three times as fast as the stomatopod punch. This is now officially the fastest known strike by any animal, relegating the stomatopod to second place.

If a trap-jaw ant snaps its jaws against the ground, it can hurl itself into a high jump of 8.3 cm or a long jump of nearly 40 cm – that's the equivalent of an average-sized human jumping 14 m high, or 40 m long. A common phenomenon when a colony of trap-jaws is disturbed is the 'popcorn effect', when ants suddenly leap in all directions, as if out of a pan of popcorn.

Record-beater

Although trap-jaw ants and stomatopods are the two fastest strikers, the animal with the fastest moving parts of all is the midge. Its wings have been recorded at 133 080 beats a minute. Their wings are so fast that they become invisible to the human eye.

*ON THE LOOKOUT
Stomatopods have incredibly complex eyes to help them track prey. They have the best colour vision of any animal, and can see about 100 000 colours, compared to a human's 10 000.*

SEE

TAKING YOUR TIME

A LOT OF ANIMALS – SUCH AS CORALS, SPONGES AND CLAMS – DON'T MOVE AT ALL, AND THAT'S AS SLOW AS YOU CAN GET. They're more or less impervious to predators, and their food comes to them, usually on ocean currents. But out of the sea and away from plankton-rich water, there tend not to be such things as stationary animals. Predators need evading, and food needs getting. There are some very slow-movers, though, and for rather similar reasons: they're largely safe from predators, and there's plenty of food where they are. Moving fast would only be a waste of energy.

Just hanging around

Probably the most thoroughly and famously slow-moving creatures are the five species of sloth, of which the best-known is the South American three-toed sloth. The animal's most likely predators would be jaguars, harpy eagles and anacondas, but it is almost always in a tree – hanging upside-down in a tree, in fact – and none of those predators seem to want to go out of their way to find it and attack. So the animal is as safe as can be expected in the wild. A sloth feeds on the leaves of the tree it's hanging in, and it eats those slowly enough to make it a rare day when it has to get down to move to another tree.

The great bulk of a sloth's life is spent sleeping: about 20 hours a day. That means that the three-toed sloth with the longest recorded lifespan of 30 years

ON GUARD Like other species of seahorse, this pygmy has highly mobile eyes to help it watch for prey and predators.

BORN TO BE SLOW This baby three-toed sloth will cling to its mother until it is about five weeks old.

spent 25 of those years asleep. When a sloth does happen to be awake it mostly eats, pulling leaves off the branch it's hanging on and moving along that branch towards more leaves at a speed that's been calculated as 14 m a minute, or 0.5 km/h. Every now and then a day comes when the leaves that are left are out of reach, and the sloth has to change trees. So it slowly descends to the ground, awkwardly stands upright and shuffles off to the next suitable tree. Sometimes there's water between the first tree and the next, and the sloth is forced to swim, which it does using a kind of dog-paddle that looks a lot more efficient than its walk.

Just as some very fast fish, normally cold-blooded animals, have come to be warm-blooded, the very slow sloth, supposedly a warm-blooded mammal, has a low body temperature. In the morning, before it can start eating, it has to warm itself in the sun, just as an insect or a reptile might. It has a slow metabolism, too, digests slowly, and urinates and defecates at the same time, just once a week – when it is obliged to come down out of the tree, dig a hole and deposit as waste a third of its body weight, because leaves are largely indigestible,.

Slowly does it

The chameleon is another very slow mover. Watching one walking along the branch of a tree, you would think it was deliberating over every single motion it made. Its eyes are slowly and independently rolling, as though it can't decide what to focus on. The front leg rises, seems to pause in the air while the chameleon contemplates whether to leave it there or put it down on the branch. It puts it down, grasps the branch, raises and lowers a hind leg, raises the other front leg, pauses, puts the leg

down, lifts its head a little and then suddenly it has an insect in its mouth. In less than the blink of an eye, the chameleon shot its tongue out over a distance two or more times its own body length, hit the insect with the tongue's tip, turned the tip into a suction cup that instantly stuck the insect to the tongue, and retracted the tongue. This wasn't a muscular action, but the release of elastic collagen tissue that had been stretched in the chameleon's mouth like a bowstring, its rolled-up tongue acting as an arrow.

Like the chameleon, which is well known for its ability to change colour, the seahorse can also camouflage itself against its background. It is also very slow. In fact, seahorses are considered the slowest swimming fish in the sea, with an average speed of 0.016 km/h. There are 25 species of them, ranging in length from 4 to 20 cm. They all live in shallows, never travel far and always return to where they started. They use their curly tails to grab onto the stems of plants to prevent them from being swept away by the current.

But the seahorse does have one very fast action. It lives on minuscule crustaceans – shrimp, crabs and the like – and as it moseys through the water, it turns its head from time to time, sticks out its snout and sucks in its prey. It can perform this suction in 5.5 milliseconds, making it one of the fastest feeding vertebrates in the world.

SPEED TRAP It takes just about 20 milliseconds for this European chameleon to catch a grasshopper with its tongue. This is one of the fastest actions in the animal kingdom, performed by one of the slowest animals.

STRIKE

CATCH

TESTS OF
STREN

GTH

2

TWO BATTLING MALE HIPPOS, MOUTHS AGAPE, REVEAL THEIR MOST FEARSOME WEAPONS – their lower canine teeth, 50 cm long, each one a deadly dentine dagger. Tests of strength take many forms in the animal kingdom, and one of them is tooth strength. Four of the most remarkable body parts on Earth are the front teeth of the beaver: chisel-sharp incisors capable of felling trees to build dams and lodges with. Sometimes physical strength has to be combined with wiliness. The leopard is strong, but not the strongest predator of the African savannah. To safeguard a kill, the leopard uses unusually strong jaw muscles to drag it up a tree, out of the reach of competing lions and hyenas. Strength ranges from little to huge, from the near-unbreakable spine of the hero shrew to the sheer brawn of the world's largest carnivores: grizzly and Kodiak bears.

BRUTE POWER

GRIZZLY BEARS ARE BIG. In fact, they and their cousins, the 3000-odd Kodiak bears living on the Kodiak islands off Alaska, are the largest land animals in the mammalian order of carnivores, which includes lions and tigers. A grizzly can stand 3 m tall on its hind legs and weigh up to 680 kg. The record weight for a Kodiak bear is colossal: 1000 kg or 1 tonne.

Although grizzlies are meat-eaters, plants make up 80 per cent of their diet, including grasses, sedges, various berries and nuts, tubers and dandelions. When they aren't eating plants, they are often eating ants, moths, mice or squirrels. It may seem strange that such a vast and powerful animal would choose such unspectacular meals, but that is part of the secret of its survival – a grizzly can eat whatever is at hand. If the season is right and the bear feels the need, it will feast on something bigger: a moose, say, or an elk, or a bison.

In fact, grizzlies are regularly seen dragging away the carcasses of animals significantly bigger than themselves. Although it is seldom possible to weigh the bear and compare its weight to that of the carcass, some hunters did once manage to do this: they found a 360 kg grizzly dragging away a 450 kg bison it had just brought down. An even more remarkable feat of bear strength was reported in the early 1900s, when a cattle-killing grizzly was caught by its leg in a spring-trap baited with a deer and chained to a tree. The bear dragged away all three – deer, trap and tree – before finally prising the trap open with its jaws.

Big brown bears

Grizzlies and Kodiak bears are North American subspecies of the brown bear, and are both significantly bigger than the Eurasian brown bear. Grizzlies are found mainly in Alaska, British Columbia in Canada and in parts of the lower 48 US states. Kodiak bears are confined to the Kodiak archipelago, where they have been cut off from other brown bears for at least 10 000 years. Normally, animals isolated on islands become smaller over the generations than the mainstream species. The Kodiak bears bucked this trend and became larger, probably because their home lies so far north – the larger the animal, the better it is at conserving heat.

Kodiaks certainly didn't need to become bigger in order to bring down bigger prey, because the only large grazing animals on their island, elk and deer, have only recently been introduced. Until then, the bears had survived through the millennia mainly on the islands' abundant supply of plants, small animals and fish. When presented with large prey, however, the Kodiak bears knew what to do, and now elk and deer are a regular part of their spring, post-hibernation diet.

GRIZZLY SNARL The face of a roaring grizzly bear is the very expression of brute power. The males are the really big ones – 1.8 times as heavy as the females. Grizzlies owe their name to the grizzled, silver-grey tips to their hairs.

BEAR SURPRISE Golfers playing a round in Big Sky, Montana, get a rude shock when a grizzly lumbers onto their course.

TUGS OF WAR

FOR A LEOPARD – BIG AND FIERCE BUT OFTEN NOT THE BIGGEST OR FIERCEST PREDATOR AROUND – MAKING A KILL IS ONLY HALF THE JOB. The other half is hanging on to it. In the parts of Africa where leopards live, there are almost always lions and hyenas too, and any leopard trying to eat its kill where it fell would almost surely be robbed. Lions steal about as much prey as they bring down, shouldering aside or killing leopards, cheetahs, jackals, wild dogs and hyenas to do so. Hyenas, in their turn, are not shy about ganging up on any of the others.

The leopard, however, has one big advantage over lions and hyenas, its two worst competitors. It can climb trees, and they can't. To keep a kill safe, the leopard drags it up into a tree, where it either eats it straight away, or stores it to feast on later. Without this strategy, the leopard would be in trouble. According to a field study in the Serengeti in Tanzania, only 5 per cent of leopard hunts were successful in the first place and they lost between 5 and 10 per cent of those kills to other predators. If they didn't have trees to retreat to, they'd be in danger of starving.

Climbing a tree with a large dead animal in your mouth is no mean feat of strength, and the secret of the leopard's carrying power is in its jaws. The strength of an animal's jaws can be judged by looking at the sagittal crest – a ridge of bone running lengthways along the top of the skull, which anchors the main chewing muscles. This is pronounced in all the big cats, wolves and wild dogs – and in anything else that needs to do heavy-duty chewing, including some leaf-eaters, such as tapirs. But it is particularly pronounced in the male leopard, because it is also the chewing muscles that an animal uses when it carries something with its teeth.

TREE STRUGGLE A literal tug of war takes place in MalaMala Game Reserve in South Africa as a leopard and a spotted hyena struggle over the carcass of a freshly killed impala.

Leopards weigh between 20 and 90 kg, and throughout Africa, they have been seen to kill some 90 species of animal. A few of these are as small as rodents or even insects, but their preferred prey are in the same weight range as themselves – animals such as impala, bushbuck and duiker – and they take on larger creatures as well. With its impressive chewing and carrying muscles, a leopard can lift three times its weight, so a giraffe calf of 100 kg or more lies well within its range. Adult eland, weighing 390-950 kg, are too heavy; even the lightest adult female eland is more than four times the weight of the heaviest leopard. But a leopard can kill and stash a young eland of 270 kg or less.

Powerful biters

Leopards are less impressive when it comes to the other set of jaw muscles. These are for biting – the force inflicted on a prey animal when it's first brought down. Researchers at the University of Sydney in Australia have worked out a formula that takes into account the dimensions of a predator's skull and jaw. In this way, they produce an estimated bite force quotient (BFQ), which allows them to compare the biting strength of various mammals, incuding extinct ones.

In the bite force quotient rankings the leopard comes in among the lowest of the cats, with a BFQ of 94. A lion scores 112, and the strongest feline bite is that of the clouded leopard – not really a leopard but a cat in a genus of its own – whose BFQ is 137. The dog with the strongest bite is the African wild dog with 142, compared to the grey wolf's 100. The spotted hyena has a BFQ of 113, the brown bear 78 and the Tasmanian devil 181, the strongest bite of any living mammal.

One mammal, however, surpassed even the Tasmanian devil: the Australian marsupial lion, which died out 40 000 years ago. It was no relation to today's African lion, except that it is thought to have looked slightly similar and to have filled roughly the same niche in the marsupial ecosystem. Its BFQ was 194.

Marsupials are more primitive than the placental mammals living on most continents today. Marsupials nourish their tiny young in pouches (the word comes from the Latin *marsupium*, for 'pouch'). Placental mammals nourish theirs for longer within their bodies via a placenta. They evolved from marsupials, but after Australia had broken away from the rest of the world's landmass. When that happened, the only mammals were marsupials, and in Australia they remained marsupials.

In time Australia came to have an African-type ecosystem, except that the grazers included such animals as the 3 m tall giant short-faced kangaroo and the hippo-sized diprotodon, which was the ancestor of today's bandicoots. The predators included the Tasmanian tiger, or thylacine, which some people believe still exists, and the marsupial lion, ancestor of today's wombats and koalas. This 'lion' – which measured 1.5 m from head to tail and weighed about 100 kg – had a bite that was not only strong but came with fearsome teeth: an enormous slicing cheek tooth and large stabbing incisors at the front. But it paid a high price for its extraordinary biting strength in the architecture of its skull. So much of the marsupial lion's skull was given over to anchoring the biting and chewing muscles that there was little room left for a brain.

When placental predators evolved, their brains grew, and with them more intelligent attack strategies and a general wiliness. That left less skullbone to anchor muscles. A leopard's ability to kill a young eland and stash it in a tree is impressive and requires considerable strength, but this is also a 'brainy' strategy – something the leopard does partly by instinct, but also because its mother taught it to do so. In effect, she imparted the information to her cubs that lions and hyenas can't climb trees.

HIGH AND DRY A leopard kill hangs high in a tree in Kenya's Masai Mara game park. The leopard has stored it there, safe from non-climbing competitors.

STOATS AND WEASELS

OF ALL CARNIVORE FAMILIES, THE LARGEST IN NUMBER AND SMALLEST IN SIZE ARE THE MUSTELIDS, THE FAMILY THAT INCLUDES FERRETS, BADGERS AND OTTERS. They are also the fiercest hunters and the most exclusively meat-eating. And among them, the most widespread group of all is the genus *Mustela* – the weasels, stoats, mink and polecats.

Mustelids are all long, slim animals, perfectly shaped to go down holes, and their favoured hunting method is generally to shoot into the burrows of mice, voles, ground squirrels and rabbits and take their prey where they live. In fact, one family member, the North American blackfooted ferret – a kind of polecat – spends its whole life in the interconnected burrows, or 'towns', of prairie dogs, a type of ground squirrel. It eats nothing else and goes nowhere else, a strategy that is no longer working

TINY FIGHTER A weasel drags a rabbit it has just killed to its lair. The weasel is the smallest of the carnivores, but is legendary for its pugnacity.

so well for it. The blackfooted ferret is now endangered because of farmers and ranchers trying to exterminate its host-cum-prey.

The blackfooted ferret lies at the extreme end of the mustelids' tendency to have a strong preference for a particular prey. Common weasels are similar but not so extreme. They eat mainly mice and voles and, in the far north, lemmings. Chasing the animals along their runways through tall grass or under snow, they take advantage of the rodents' instinctive reluctance to break cover and expose themselves to birds such as kestrels. (This could be seen as a slightly perverse instinct because if a mouse were able to figure odds, it would know that there is less chance of being caught by a kestrel that may not be there than by a weasel that definitely is.)

If mice and voles are always in abundance in a particular common weasel's territory, it is content to eat nothing else. But if shortages occur – and rodents can be seasonal – it will switch to rabbits or birds. At its largest, a common weasel usually has a top weight of about 90 g and a length of about 20 cm, but it is quite capable of killing a rabbit far larger than itself, maybe several times larger, and dragging it back to its lair.

The mustelid share-out

Generally speaking, however, in the mustelid share-out, rabbits are reserved for stoats, which are larger than weasels. In many parts of the world – almost anywhere in the north of the northern temperate zone – weasels and stoats coexist without competing for prey. If there is anywhere a shortage of rodents, there tends to be a corresponding shortage of weasels, and if lagomorphs (rabbits and hares) are lacking, stoats are usually low in numbers.

It sometimes happens that a particular location will have stoats or weasels but not both, even though there are both rabbits and mice. Then a strange thing occurs: the predator becomes a convenient median size, so that it can take on both kinds of prey – it can get down the smaller mouse holes and still easily take rabbits. In other words, weasels get bigger or stoats get smaller. For example, there are no stoats in southern Europe or North Africa, but in both regions the weasels grow up to 24 cm long and weigh up to 250 g – not quite as large as a northern European stoat, but close. Conversely, there are no weasels in Northern Ireland, and the stoats there are only slightly larger than, say, mainland British weasels.

Smallest and purest

The common weasel's alternative name is 'least weasel', because it is the smallest mustelid. It is the smallest carnivore and also among the purest – unlike some dogs and bears, also carnivores, a weasel never resorts to eating plants. If a weasel ever scavenges, it is out of desperation, because it normally likes its meat freshly killed. Its main challenge in pursuit of prey is locating a mouse or vole underground or a lemming under snow, but once it has got a rodent in its sights, the animal is normally as good as dead. This contrasts with a big carnivore such as a leopard, which has to get by on a 5 per cent kill rate.

WOLVERINE

THE WOLVERINE IS THE BIGGEST MUSTELID AND, FOR ITS SIZE, A MOST FEROCIOUS AND EFFICIENT MEAT-EATER. This large cousin of the weasel grows up to about 1 m long and weighs up to 16 kg. It is robust and muscular, and frequently tackles prey far larger than itself.

Wolverines live in the far north of all northern continents and occupy vast territories – roughly one animal for 180 km². Because of the remoteness of the places where they live, relatively little is known about them – all attempts to count their numbers have failed. What is known for certain is that they are ferocious. Elliott Coues, a 19th-century American naturalist, wrote about the wolverine's 'supernatural cunning' and called it 'a terror to all other beasts'. Wolverines have been known to bring down elk and reindeer by leaping on their backs, holding on tight and tearing at the animal's neck until it stumbles and is then finished off. They have then defended the resulting meal from wolves and grizzly bears.

One of several other names for the wolverine is skunk bear, because it looks a bit like a bear and because, like a skunk, it has two stripes from its shoulders to its tail and releases a smelly musk when under pressure. Its scientific name is *Gulo gulo*, which means 'glutton glutton' in Latin – *gulo* is repeated, not to emphasise the animal's gluttony, but because it is the only animal in its genus.

Unlike weasels, wolverines are also scavengers – in fact, they may get most of their food by scavenging other predators' kills. It is almost certain that they have no predators themselves. In fact, the only animal known to have killed a wolverine is a porcupine – by inadvertently stabbing its aggressor in the stomach with its sharp quills.

ORDER: Carnivora

FAMILY: Mustelidae

SPECIES: *Gulo gulo* – also called skunk bear and carcajou

HABITAT: Far northern parts of North America, Europe and Asia

KEY FEATURES: Extremely ferocious scavenger and predator, one that habitually fights above its weight

AERIAL
WEIGHT-LIFTERS

A female harpy eagle can weigh up to about 10 kg, so if she is carrying an 8 kg two-toed sloth, she is putting a weight of 18 kg on her wings.

BIRD VERSUS PREY A golden eagle swoops down on a hare in the snow-clad uplands of Kazakhstan. Hunters in the Central Asian republic keep and train golden eagles to catch game. This bird is taking part in a traditional hunting contest.

THE MOST IMPRESSIVE AERIAL WEIGHT-LIFTERS ARE THE LARGE EAGLES, whose wings often have to support the weight not only of the birds themselves but also of their prey. Of these, the biggest in most measurable dimensions (except length of wing, which the golden eagle wins) is the Philippine eagle, up to 1 m long. The heaviest is the South American harpy eagle, which preys on a variety of large animals including sloths, big fish and howler monkeys. A female harpy can weigh up to about 10 kg, so if she is carrying an 8 kg two-toed sloth, she is putting a weight of 18 kg on her wings.

Weight on wings

If an animal is going to fly, it needs to be light. The world's heaviest flying bird is the African kori bustard, which weighs up to about 19 kg, but whenever possible it simply avoids taking to its wings. If chased by a predator, it tries to run away before making any attempt at flight. If it does comes to that last resort, a lot of ponderous and strenuous-looking flapping precedes takeoff and it doesn't stay airborne for long. Kori bustards are, in fact, on the cusp of flightlessness. If evolution pushes a bird all the way in that direction, it can let itself go weight-wise. The heaviest bird in the world today is the non-flying ostrich, which weighs up to 160 kg.

Among birds that are serious about flying, the weight limit is about 15 kg, which takes in Andean condors (the largest, as opposed to heaviest, of all flying birds, with a wing span of up to 3.1 m), wandering albatrosses and swans. The last two specialise in long-distance wind-sailing, while Andean condors spend most of their day riding high mountain thermals. None of the three is a bird of prey. Their wings have only to support the weight of the birds themselves.

With an eagle, it is easy to see the effort it has to make to keep flying in the moments after it has caught an animal. Until then, it may have been soaring or diving, but now it is almost stalled. It dips a little as it seems to put every muscle in its body into the first pump of the wings, and then it keeps on pumping until either it gets to a spot where it can stop and eat or it makes it all the way to its nest and chicks. Sometimes,

even if the eagle is on its way to the nest, it will stop anyway, cut the meat up and make two or three trips – but that often leads to losing part of a hard-earned meal.

Fearsome feet

Other than its wings, a bird of prey's most important tools are its talons, used to subdue, as well as carry, prey. The grasp is mortally tight; the claws stab and normally the animal dies of shock as much as anything else by the time the bird is ready to eat it. Talons have two different configurations. Eagles and hawks have three toes pointing forward and one, thumb-like, pointing backward. Owls and ospreys have two pointing forward and two back. That, at least, is the default position. An owl or osprey can rotate one of the backward-facing toes to face forward. This probably gives owls extra flexibility in grasping prey when hunting by night, and it may do something similar for the osprey, which catches slippery fish.

Condors are vultures – that is, scavengers. They spot something dead, descend on it and then eat it where it fell; they don't have to carry anything. As a result, their feet are large, padded and splayed to help them walk on and in carcasses. There is, however, a vulture that does carry things: the lammergeier, or bearded vulture, whose range stretches across mountainous areas in southern Europe, Africa, India and Tibet. It descends on carcasses the way any other vulture does, but instead of eating the rotting flesh, it goes straight to the bones, cracks them and scoops out the marrow. Some 90 per cent of the lammergeier's diet is bone marrow, and it tries to get all the marrow the carcass has to offer.

When a bone is too big for the vulture to crack with its beak, the bird picks it up with its feet, tucks it up against its body and flies away with it to a bone-cracking stone, or ossuary. This is usually a large flat rock near its nest, which it uses regularly. The lammergeier glides downwind at 60-80 km/h, carrying the bone, then goes into a steeper dive, takes one foot off the bone and at an altitude of about 60 m drops it on to the rock. The bone

FISH FEAST A white-tailed eagle – also called a sea eagle – clutches a fish it has caught. This Old World eagle, which is closely related to the North American bald eagle, preys on other birds and small mammals as well as fish, and also scavenges the catches of other predators, such as otters.

cracks, and the lammergeier swoops down and gets the marrow.

Thunderbirds

Truly vast flying birds did once exist: the teratorns, whose fossils have been found in Argentina and California. Four species have been discovered, all of them roughly two and a half times the size of a condor, weighing 80 kg with an 8 m wingspan. Wings that large would have been physically impossible to flap, and so they probably held them out, caught the wind and soared across the countryside grabbing land animals the way an albatross grabs fish from the sea.

The teratorns did not exist in a dinosaur-distant past. They became extinct between 40 000 and 11 000 years ago and would have been around recently enough for humans conceivably to have seen them – or to have been snatched by them. They could even be connected to Native American legends about the great thunderbird, a wrathful and terrifying creature, representations of which often appear on totem poles. It was believed to cause thunder and create the winds by the beating of its vast wings.

GNAWERS AND BORERS

ALL ANIMALS LIVE BY INGESTING THINGS THAT ARE ALIVE OR RECENTLY HAVE BEEN. To do this, many of the higher animals – mammals in particular, but also many reptiles and fish – need cutting and grinding tools: teeth. How many teeth an animal needs, what kind, how big and how sharp vary so much among species that an expert can usually identify particular animals by those characteristics alone.

Mammal teeth are all made of the same substances, and most have the same constituent parts. The basic structure is a pulp cavity enclosed by hard dentine, which is covered above the gum by an even harder substance, enamel – in fact, the body's hardest substance of all. But in mammals (unlike non-mammals, whose teeth are all basically the same, just different sizes), the teeth have different

MIGHTY GNAWERS Using these four teeth, its incisors, the beaver can fell trees as effectively as any human with an axe or chainsaw. Because the beaver's incisors continue to grow, it has to keep using them to maintain them at the right length – 25 mm exposed above the gums.

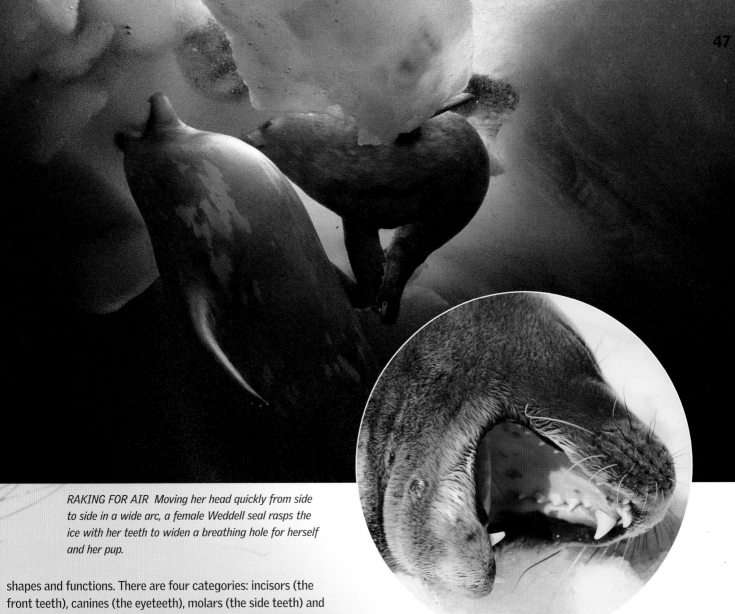

RAKING FOR AIR *Moving her head quickly from side to side in a wide arc, a female Weddell seal rasps the ice with her teeth to widen a breathing hole for herself and her pup.*

shapes and functions. There are four categories: incisors (the front teeth), canines (the eyeteeth), molars (the side teeth) and premolars (transitional teeth between the canines and the molars). The canines are for biting, the molars do the chewing, while gnawing is where the incisors come into their own.

The way each type is emphasised in an animal's mouth reflects what it eats and how it gets what it eats. Nobody today has seen a sabre-tooth cat in action, but one look at its skull and teeth indicates what it did. Either it chased large animals, caught and stabbed them, or it ambushed and stabbed them.

Incisive incisors

Gnawing is what rodents do – their name comes from the Latin for 'gnaw' – and the world's most spectacular gnawing incisors of all belong to the beaver, the largest rodent in North America, Europe and Asia. Wielding these magnificent natural tools, beavers gnaw down trees – mainly aspens, poplars, cottonwoods and willows – to build their dams and lodges, cutting them as neatly as any human with a hand-axe might. In fact, archaeologists have discovered an ancient Native American cutting tool made out of a beaver's incisor.

Rodents are such specialists in gnawing that they have only two types of teeth: incisors and molars. The molars are much like human molars, and once grown, they're there, with roots. The four incisors, however, do not have roots. The pulp

ICE-PICK TEETH *The Weddell seal has uniquely angled canines and incisors that have adapted to gnaw through ice. The sharp teeth are also used to catch and hold on to prey such as fish and octopus, which the seal swallows in large chunks without chewing.*

CARNIVORE TEETH

CROWN

ROOT

A JAGUAR'S CANINE TOOTH

Of the four types of mammal teeth, the most important to a typical carnivore, or meat-eater, such as a jaguar, are the canines. These four long teeth at the front of the mouth – two top and two bottom – are used to grip and kill prey quickly. The incisors strip flesh from bones. Carnivores also have specially adapted molars called carnassials that are used to shear off chunks of meat.

PIDDOCK

THE MOST IMPRESSIVE

BORER OF THEM ALL IS THE COMMON PIDDOCK, WHICH CAN PENETRATE ROCK. This small bivalve is a marine mollusc (snail relative) with a long, hinged double shell that bores holes. In fact, there are many different piddocks living in holes in different substances. Tiny ones make their homes by boring into the shells of other molluscs, such as oysters. Some, such as the great piddock, which is 8 cm long, bore into wood and limestone.

For a simple mollusc, boring into rock is an amazing feat – all the more so because the piddock has no teeth. Its secret is a small, slow start. A common piddock begins life as a larva, which swims around and finds a suitable rock to settle on. It then changes into its adult bivalve form and starts to bore down into the rock to make its home. It does this by using the serrated edges of its tiny double shell as a file. Gripping the rock with its foot, it twists and grinds – the harder the rock, the slower the process, and the slower the piddock grows. To bore a hole 5 cm deep in hard rock may take several years.

Living within a rock hole provides much better protection than a shell, and the piddock can feed by extending its neck-like double siphon out of the hole, filtering in water with oxygen and food – tiny marine creatures – on one side and getting rid of waste water on the other. It can't move, however. Having excavated its living quarters to fit, the piddock is locked in its hole for life. When it eventually dies, its legacy is a valuable hiding place, quickly occupied by another marine creature, such as a crab or a small fish.

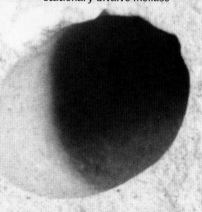

CLASS: Bivalva
ORDER: Myoida
SPECIES: Common piddock, *Pholas dactylus*
HABITAT: Lives in the sea in holes drilled mainly in rock
DISTRIBUTION: Atlantic coast from Britain south to Spain and Morocco, the Mediterranean and Black Sea
KEY FEATURES: A permanently stationary bivalve mollusc

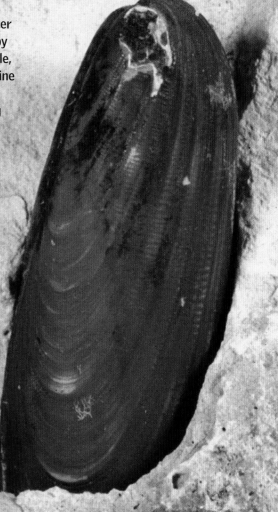

cavity remains open, like a hair follicle, and like hair a rodent's incisors keep on growing. From the time a rat, for example, is ten days old, its incisors grow at a rate of about 13 cm a year, completely replacing themselves every 40 to 50 days.

This means that a rodent has to keep gnawing, because if it didn't wear its incisors down in this way, they would grow through its palate and impede its ability to eat. The busy beaver is busy because it has no choice – its teeth force it to work. Although you aren't likely to hear the phrase 'as busy as a rat', the same applies. Rats are not big enough to fell trees, but they can gnaw through almost anything, up to and including lead.

Another difference between rodents and other mammals is that rodents' incisors have enamel only at the front. As the rodent gnaws, moving its teeth back and forth, it wears away the softer dentine on the back of the incisor, creating an extremely sharp chisel of a tooth, the better to keep gnawing with.

Gnawing at ice

The Weddell seal is another prodigious mammal gnawer. Around the coasts of Antarctica, when winter approaches, the sea ice grows outward very quickly, sometimes at a rate of kilometres a day. Most Antarctic animals – including penguins, killer whales and leopard seals – stay in the water ahead of the ice's leading edge. But Weddell seals let the ice spread out over them. The water underneath the ice is always about –1°C, the same temperature as Antarctic water anywhere. It is quite warm enough to survive in, and while the ice spreads there are no more killer whales or predatory leopard seals to prey on the seals.

But Weddell seals still need air to breathe. Tidal movements, especially during the summer and near the shore, make the ice crack in places, and the Weddell seals enlarge parts of these cracks into round, head-and-shoulder-sized breathing holes. During the winter, they keep them open by gnawing the constantly re-forming ice. It is not a perfect solution, however. The Weddell seal is not a rodent, and as the seasons pass its teeth wear down. When it can't cut the ice any more, the seal dies.

TEETH OR TUSKS?

SOMETIMES TEETH GET SO OUT OF PROPORTION THAT THEY CEASE TO BE USED AS NORMAL TEETH. The white Arctic whale, the narwhal, has two teeth in its upper jaw, and in the male, the left-hand tooth points forwards and grows outwards in an anticlockwise twist until it is 2-3 m long. It has become a tusk, which it uses as a lance when it spars with other males. It is very like the horn of the mythical unicorn and may have contributed to the legend.

Walruses also have tusks that are elongated canines. The males use them in sparring, and both sexes use them to drag their bodies across a beach – for this reason the walrus was once

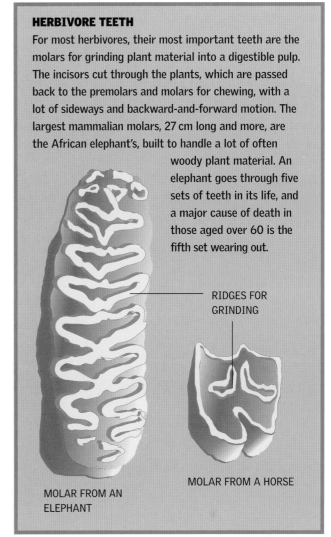

HERBIVORE TEETH

For most herbivores, their most important teeth are the molars for grinding plant material into a digestible pulp. The incisors cut through the plants, which are passed back to the premolars and molars for chewing, with a lot of sideways and backward-and-forward motion. The largest mammalian molars, 27 cm long and more, are the African elephant's, built to handle a lot of often woody plant material. An elephant goes through five sets of teeth in its life, and a major cause of death in those aged over 60 is the fifth set wearing out.

RIDGES FOR GRINDING

MOLAR FROM AN ELEPHANT

MOLAR FROM A HORSE

known as the 'toothwalker'. The largest teeth of all are the African elephant's incisors or tusks. Again, males spar with them, but both sexes have them and employ them in conjunction with the trunk as strong and handy appendages for moving and carrying things. The heaviest recorded tooth of any living species was an African elephant tusk of unknown origin, weighed in Paris in 1900 – it hit 117 kg on the scales.

RAT MARKS A piece of lead piping shows the marks where a rat has gnawed at it.

INNER STRENGTH

THE HERO SHREW LOOKS LIKE MANY OTHER LARGE SHREWS. A native of the forests of Rwanda, Uganda and Congo, it has thick woolly grey fur, measures between 12 and 15 cm and weighs between 30 and 115 g. But the Mangbetu people of Congo will point out that in one respect at least it is not like other large shrews. To show the difference, a Mangbetu man will stand with one foot on a hero shrew's back and the other foot in the air. In a while, he'll get off, and the shrew will wander away.

Any other mammal that size would be crushed by the weight, but the hero shrew does not even seem to notice it. That is because of its remarkable spine. In other small mammals, the spine accounts for about 0.5 per cent of body weight; in a hero shrew it is four per cent. Its spine is extremely flexible, with joints in places where other mammals have never had them. Each vertebra in the lumbar region – between the ribcage and the hips – is a large, corrugated cylinder with a complex of interlocking

BIONIC FISH It may not look like a fish, but it is – a yellow boxfish, which lives in reefs in the Pacific and Indian oceans. It starts life a bright canary yellow, but this softens with age to a more mustard colour. The surprisingly streamlined fish inspired the design of the Mercedes-Benz Bionic car.

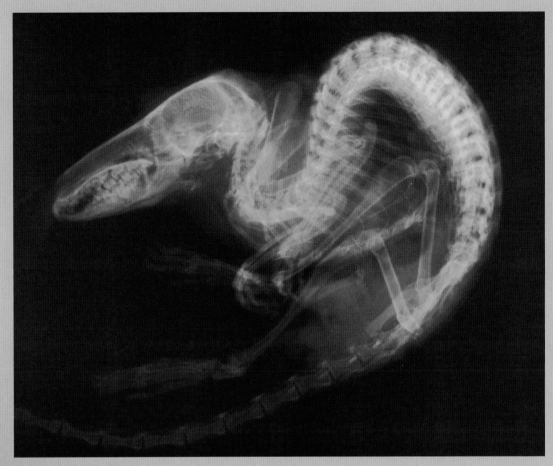

HEROIC LOAD BEARER An X-ray reveals the extraordinarily large backbone of the Central African hero shrew. This is so strong that the shrew can support 1000 times its body mass placed on its back – equivalent to ten elephants loaded onto the back of an adult human.

tubercules, like a mass of cables. As for the spinal muscles, the transverse ones (the ones that inhibit flexibility) are weaker than in other animals, while the flexion and extension muscles (the lengthways ones) are stronger.

Unfortunately, most scientific observation of hero shrews has been of captive ones. Scientists know *what* makes the shrew's backbone so strong, but they don't know *why* it needs one like that. From the few studies done in the wild, the shrew does not appear to burrow or hunt things in burrows, which would explain the need for a strong, snake-like backbone. Like any other shrew, it feeds on insects, earthworms and small frogs. What the hero shrew's spine does demonstrate, however, is the extreme toughness and strength possible in small animals.

Armour plating

Many people will have seen animals such as ticks, horseflies and small cockroaches, which because of their compactness and tough exoskeletons (external skeletons), seem sometimes to be impervious to swatting or squashing. A more unusual animal that uses external armour plating is the boxfish.

Fish are vertebrates with backbones and ribs, so they don't have exoskeletons. Generally, they are supple, allowing them to move their bodies and tails from side to side for propulsion.

> **Because of its design, the boxfish creates some of the same currents that account for the high speed of delta-wing aircraft, including Concorde.**

Boxfish, however, are different. They are a group of brightly coloured reef fish ranging in size from very small to about 60 cm long, and none of them looks as though it could possibly swim. They have given up the usual suppleness of fish and, while keeping the internal skeleton, have developed an external one as well. Bony carapaces cover up to three-quarters of a boxfish's body, leaving just the head and tail with the normal fishy outer skin. Viewed end on, they are shaped like triangles, squares or pentagons.

The chief purpose of this armour is probably to protect the boxfish from the teeth of bigger fish – many also secrete poisons just to make sure. But surprisingly, their shape does not impede their ability to swim. Instead, it takes them into a new dimension of swimming. All that moves on a boxfish is the tip of its tail and its fins, and yet it moves very well. Researchers made an epoxy resin model of one and put it in a water tunnel illuminated by lasers. They discovered that swirls or vortices developed around the model and the design created some of the same currents that account for the high speed of delta-wing aircraft, including Concorde. The DaimlerChrysler car company drew on these discoveries to create the Mercedes-Benz Bionic car based on the lines of a boxfish. In wind tunnel tests it achieved a very low drag coefficient, and at 90 km/h uses only 2.6 litres of fuel per 100 km.

MIGHT
RI

IS
GHT
3

A RESEARCH DINGHY IS DWARFED BY THE AWESOME PROPORTIONS OF A BLUE WHALE IN THE WATERS OFF SANTA BARBARA, CALIFORNIA. At about 27 m long and 190 tonnes, the blue whale is the world's largest animal. Other superlatives follow from its monumental size. Its heart alone is the size of a small car and its tongue weighs around 3 tonnes. It gives birth to the world's largest baby, weighing 2-3 tonnes. It has the world's loudest voice, carrying for thousands of kilometres. It also has the biggest appetite: each day it strains 3.6 tonnes of tiny, shrimp-like krill out of the seawater with its baleen plates, which the blue whale and its relatives have instead of teeth. That's around 40 million krill a day. Another of the blue whale's records is the largest discrepancy between the size of a predator and the size of its prey.

A QUESTION OF SIZE

NATURE THROWS UP SOME SPECTACULAR VARIATIONS IN SIZE, SOMETIMES BETWEEN CREATURES THAT ARE OTHERWISE SIMILAR. Take the blue whale and Kitti's hog-nosed bat. Both are mammals, so both have a lineage that includes whatever dinosaur-dodging, weasel-like creature was the first mammal. They are both warm-blooded, and the young of both feed on their mothers' milk. Neither of them is a conventional mammal in that, instead of walking on the ground, one swims like a fish and the other flies like a bird. But there is one significant difference between them: the blue whale has a top weight of 190 tonnes, unlike Kitti's hog-nosed bat, otherwise known as the bumblebee bat, which weighs only 3 g at most. The blue whale, the biggest mammal on Earth, is 6.3 million times heavier than the smallest, the bumblebee bat.

Then there's Cuba's bee hummingbird. It descends from the dinosaurs, has warm blood and feathers and lays eggs. The same can be said of the world's largest bird, the ostrich, but one weighs just 1.8 g while the other weighs 160 kg. Besides being smallest and largest, both birds break other records. The ostrich lays the biggest egg, about the size of a basketball; the bee hummingbird lays the smallest, the size of a pea. The ostrich is the fastest running bird, at 72 km/h; the bee hummingbird has the fastest wingbeat, at 80 beats a second, rising to 200 during courtship display. The hummingbird also has the fewest feathers of any bird and the highest body temperature at 40°C, dropping to 19° at night.

BUMBLEBEE BAT Kitti's hog-nosed bat, which lives along the River Kwai in Thailand, is around 3 cm long and has the smallest skull of any mammal. The tiny bat, which was first discovered in 1973, is an endangered species.

The blue whale, the biggest mammal on Earth, is 6.3 million times heavier than the smallest, the bumblebee bat.

UNDER THE MICROSCOPE The tiny, rootless Wolffia arrhiza, one of the species of duckweed, floats on the surface of quiet streams and ponds. Being small means that the Wolffia duckweeds are easily spread. They're probably carried around on waterbirds' feet. They are also blown in winds and some have been found in the water of melted hailstones.

Plant comparisons

The tallest flowering plant is an Australian eucalyptus, the mountain ash, the tallest recorded specimen of which was measured in 1881 – after being felled – at a towering 114.3 m. At the other end of the scale, the smallest flowering plants are the 11 species of duckweed in the genus *Wolffia*, the second smallest of which is also found in Australia. The very smallest of them all, *W. globosa*, is found everywhere in the tropics. The *Wolffia* duckweeds are so small they are called 'watermeal' – thousands of them together feel like slightly coarse, wet flour. The average individual *W. globosa* plant measures just 0.6 mm long and 0.3 mm wide and weighs 150 micrograms, about as much as two grains of salt.

Being a flowering plant, *W. globosa* produces flowers, but you need a microscope to see them. The flower sits in a cavity on the upper side of the plant's body and has one pistil and one stamen; a bouquet of, say, a dozen of these, along with their parent plants, can fit on a pinhead. After a *globosa* flower has been pollinated, it produces the world's smallest fruit. This has one seed and is called a utricle.

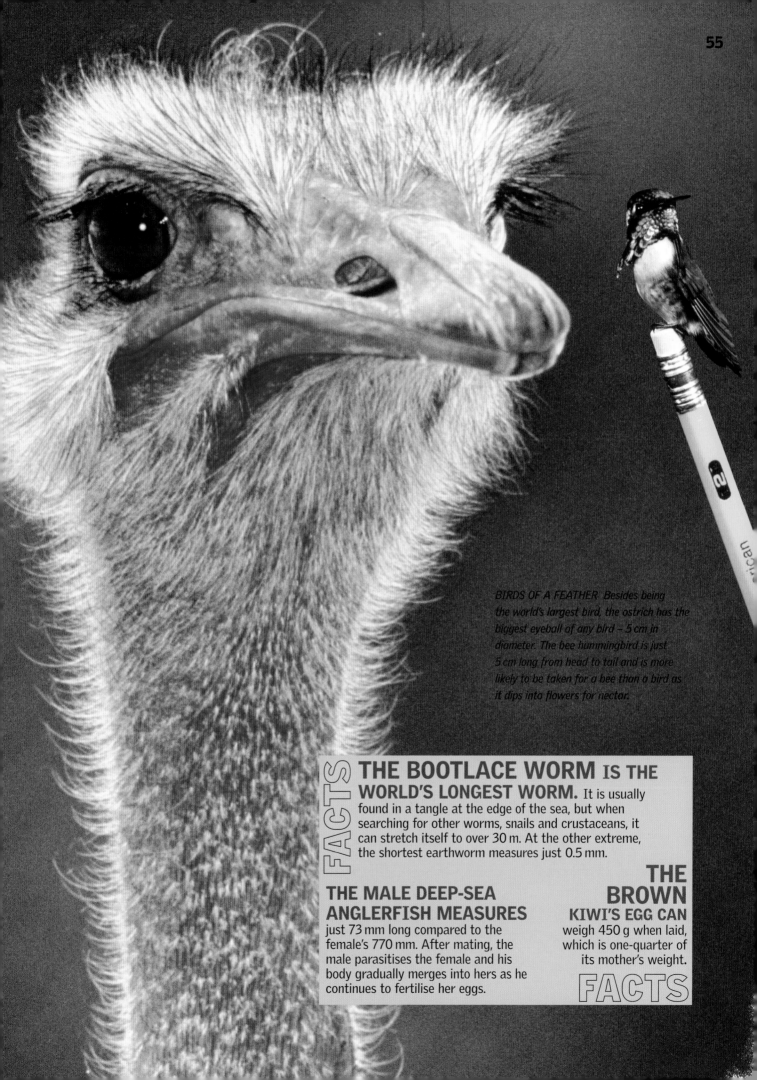

BIRDS OF A FEATHER Besides being the world's largest bird, the ostrich has the biggest eyeball of any bird – 5 cm in diameter. The bee hummingbird is just 5 cm long from head to tail and is more likely to be taken for a bee than a bird as it dips into flowers for nectar.

FACTS

THE BOOTLACE WORM IS THE **WORLD'S LONGEST WORM.** It is usually found in a tangle at the edge of the sea, but when searching for other worms, snails and crustaceans, it can stretch itself to over 30 m. At the other extreme, the shortest earthworm measures just 0.5 mm.

THE MALE DEEP-SEA ANGLERFISH MEASURES just 73 mm long compared to the female's 770 mm. After mating, the male parasitises the female and his body gradually merges into hers as he continues to fertilise her eggs.

THE BROWN KIWI'S EGG CAN weigh 450 g when laid, which is one-quarter of its mother's weight.

FACTS

WHY BE BIG?

INSTEAD OF CATCHING ONE FISH AT A TIME, a humpback whale, after helping round up a whole shoal, opens its mouth and gulps most of the shoal down. The humpback can do this because it is 16 m long and weighs 65 tonnes. Spinner dolphins – which are each only about 2 m long, weigh 75 kg and could easily fit whole into a humpback's mouth – also round up shoals of fish. But whereas the spinner dolphins gang up on the fish in teams of hundreds, it takes only a dozen or fewer humpbacks to do the same thing.

The humpbacks blow a wall of bubbles in front of the fish or a large column of bubbles around them. Then they herd the fish towards

BIG CATCH A humpback whale rises to the surface to devour its prey.

the bubbles by shouting at them in a way that only humpback whales can shout. The frightened fish won't swim through the bubbles but instead go straight up the wall or through the column to the surface, while humpbacks surge behind and gobble them up wholesale.

The spinners, on their hunt, work themselves into a frenzy, leaping out of the water as they approach the shoal, turning sideways somersaults and then surrounding the shoal, forcing it to the surface with their own bodies and eating the fish, one fish to one dolphin at a time. It looks tiring, and you have to wonder if the spinners are really getting enough energy from their catch to cover the energy they expend catching them.

As for the fish, they really do suffer from not being bigger. Compare them, panicking and dying in their shoals, with the world's largest fish, the whale shark. This animal has no predators. It spends its days gliding through the oceans and filtering out plankton. Life is easy. The same is true of the largest whale, the blue, which does exactly the same as the whale shark. In both cases, it is as though evolution has brought the two species through all the hectic, tooth-and-claw stages of existence and finally got them to retirement size – the size of no more worries.

Size matters

In the 1890s, an American palaeontologist named Edward Drinker Cope suggested in a paper that there is a tendency for all evolving organisms to increase in size over time. By the 1970s, Cope's Rule had been all but dismissed, but a 2007 study seems to have gone

some way to redeeming it. Two researchers have analysed 65 pairs of related dinosaurs, each pair separated by millions of years, and found that, on average, the more recent dinosaurs were 25 per cent bigger than the older ones.

While there are some advantages or consolations in being small, the very general picture is one of most species – over a massive time scale – straining to get bigger and to enjoy the perks of being big. And what are those perks? Probably the most important is freedom from predation. That freedom isn't total, and the young are usually exempt, but for the biggest animals the threat of getting killed and eaten is rare.

For many of the very big animals – although not the whale shark and the blue whale – diets have become more varied. The food-selection possibilities broadened as the animals got bigger. This is especially true of predators – and as species get bigger they're better at competing for food and for the territories that contain it. Big animals also tend to live longer and, because of their bigger brains, are usually more intelligent. They are better able to survive hard times, too.

Within a species, the biggest individuals are usually the better breeders, which is actually the mechanism by which Cope's Rule operates: the big ones are the parents of the next generation, so the whole species imperceptibly grows.

Lucky predator

One of the winners in the size stakes is the estuarine or saltwater crocodile, the world's largest crocodile. It is found in and around Australia and most of the southwestern Pacific. Males can be up to 6 m long, females up to 3 m, and the biggest males can weigh half a tonne, making it the world's largest reptile of any kind.

Nothing preys on a saltwater croc, and a large one eats anything it can catch, from small crustaceans to dingos, wallabies, shore birds, wild boar, monkeys, cows, horses and the occasional human. This creature has capitalised on the absence of predators and the open-ended diet to enjoy all the advantages of bigness – with the possible exception of enhanced intelligence (but who knows?). It also misses out on at least one of the disadvantages of being large: it doesn't have to eat if it doesn't want to. A crocodile is cold-blooded, so gets its warmth from the warmth of the air. It only needs to eat about once a week. Otherwise, it can just lie still, basking in the sun. It is probably as close to perfection as an animal can get.

Soup of the day

The world's largest arachnid (animals that include spiders and scorpions) is the goliath bird-eating spider. Found in South America, it is 10 cm long and has a legspan of 26 cm – the size of a standard dinner plate. All the bird-eating spiders are large tarantulas and have been known to kill nestling birds. Their usual food, though, is a large insect, most often a beetle. To get their prey, bird-eating spiders don't bother with the usual spider trickery – webs, trap-doors and the like – they just stalk their meals and pounce, inject venom with their 25 mm fangs and wait for the animal to die. Then the spider regurgitates digestive juices that reduce the victim's soft parts to a kind of soup, which it drinks.

WEB-LESS HUNTER
A young bird has become the victim of a bird-eating spider. These spiders do not make a web to catch food, they pounce on their prey and inject a deadly venom. They can also kill frogs, small snakes, lizards and bats.

Marabou stork

One bird that illustrates the advantages of size is Africa's marabou stork. If New World vultures are thought to be storks, this is an Old World stork that's definitely a vulture. It has some of the standard vulture characteristics – the mainly bald head and back of the neck (the better for rooting around in bloody carcasses as a feathered head would soon become matted with blood) and a meat-cleaver bill. The head isn't totally bald. There are some wispy feathers on it, and the skin is somewhere in the range

MIGHTY WINGS The marabou stork is an accomplished and graceful flyer, with hollow leg and toe bones to reduce its weight during flight.

LARGEST REPTILE A saltwater crocodile can snap up just about anything that comes into its range, including this kangaroo.

of pink to magenta, with darker pigmentation resembling liver spots on the face and upper portion of the bill. In the breeding season, the spots on the face become encrusted with dried blood.

This big bird stands up to 1.5 m tall and weighs about 9 kg. Its wingspan is about 3 m and it flies easily, covering great distances from one scavenging spot to another. It has no predators – vultures seldom do – has a wide choice of food, both living and dead, and seems to have no fear of anything, including people. Groups of storks hang around fishing villages and slaughterhouses, and they mass on rubbish dumps. One report describes marabous standing a few feet from abbatoir workers cleaning carcasses, patiently waiting for scraps. The birds also gather near grass fires, ready to swoop on animals fleeing the flames.

Giant frog

The world's largest frog is the goliath frog of Cameroon in West Africa. It can grow to a length of 32 cm, not counting the legs, and it can weigh 3.3 kg. Its diet consists of anything that will fit into its mouth, mainly fish and various invertebrates. It has no vocal sacs and so can't croak; instead, what the male does at courting time is to open his mouth ever so slightly and whistle.

The goliath frog certainly lives up to its name, but it raises the question, why do frogs stop there? Why are there no bigger ones? Well, this is an example of a type of animal reaching its physical limit. A frog is an amphibian, and amphibians breathe through their skin. They have lungs, but those only help them breathe in air, and even then frogs still get half their oxygen and release 70 per cent of their carbon dioxide by way of their skin; under water, the skin handles the entire gas exchange. As an animal grows, its surface area shrinks in relation to the volume of its body. In the case of the big frog, this is a major drawback – that much skin can provide only enough oxygen to service that much frog and no more.

There is a bigger amphibian than the goliath frog – the Chinese giant salamander, which can weigh over 50 kg. It lives in temperate places with cold water, and cold water holds more oxygen than warm water. There were also much bigger amphibians during the Carboniferous period, between 345 and 280 million years ago, but there appears to have been more oxygen in air and water then.

LEAP FROG The goliath frog is said to be able to make 2 m leaps, but that after three leaps it is exhausted and has to rest.

The downside

Being big, of course, does come with a few disadvantages. The young of larger animals take longer to be born and then to grow up. Large animals can't have throwaway offspring, flooding the world with eggs and gambling that some will survive. Instead, they have only a few babies and have to take good care of them. Another disadvantage is that, with exceptions like the saltwater crocodile, having acquired the ability to get more food, big creatures now have to get it or starve.

Under the analysis of Cope's Rule, one of the drawbacks of great size is that big animals are the first to disappear in a mass extinction event. Many people now believe that man is affecting life on Earth with the same force as whatever it was that wiped out the dinosaurs. By 1967 hunters had reduced the blue whale population to just 1000, while the African elephant was brought close to extinction by ivory traders. The largest bird in North America, the California condor, with a wingspan of around 3 m, was reduced to just 25 at one point by shooting, poisoning and loss of habitat. The world's largest carnivore, the polar bear, is expected to be among the first victims of global warming. The largest cat, the tiger, is on the verge of being wiped out for its skin and the value of its body parts in Chinese medicine. The goliath frog is very hard to find these days as a result of people eating it or selling it to collectors – some westerners are said to pay $3000 dollars for one.

Even those fiercest of predators, the saltwater crocodiles, are regularly shot, often in reprisal for something they ate. However, these crocs don't actually seem to be endangered, which is appropriate: crocodiles are the largest reptiles to have survived the last mass extinction.

THE LARGEST AFRICAN ELEPHANT EVER MEASURED WAS A BULL KILLED IN ANGOLA IN 1955.

It weighed 10 tonnes and was 4 m high at the shoulder. Apart from being the world's largest land animal, the African elephant holds numerous other size records. It has the largest ears and teeth – its tusks – of any land mammal. Its trunk is around 1.5 m long and weighs 135 kg. It has the largest brain, with an average weight of 4.8 kg compared to a human's 1.3–1.4 kg. The usual way of using brain size to estimate intelligence is by comparing it to the animal's body size and by that measure the human wins, but elephants' intelligence is still impressive. They are highly social animals with relationships and rules of behaviour. During its lifetime – which can be over 60 years – an elephant stores memories of such things as droughts, routes to waterholes, good feeding spots and dangerous situations. Elephants that raid farms always know to do it when the farmers are asleep, and when they reach a reserve's boundary, they know there's danger beyond and will stop and turn around. It seems that there is truth in the saying 'elephants never forget'.

CLASS: Mammalia
ORDER: Proboscidea
SPECIES: *Loxodonta africana*
HABITAT: Forest, bush, savannah
DISTRIBUTION: Sub-Saharan Africa
KEY FEATURES: World's largest land animal, with the longest gestation period at 22 months

AFRICAN
ELEPHANT

When a male emperor penguin arrives at the breeding ground it is at its annual fattest and it can store surplus food in its digestive system, releasing it little by little.

WHEN THE ANTARCTIC WINTER APPROACHES AND THE FIRST AUTUMN STORMS COME IN, THE MAMMALS AND BIRDS THAT HAVE SPENT THE SUMMER off the edge of the iceshelf set off north to islands or to waters that they know will not freeze. Among them are the different species of Antarctic penguin – with one famous exception. The emperor penguins stay put. In fact, they even take a little hike south, towards the continental coast, so that they can be sure they're on ice that won't melt in the spring. Why? Because by spring they'll have chicks that will have hatched but will not yet be ready to swim.

That means that the adults – the adult males, as it happens – will be spending the winter in the coldest place on Earth. Emperor penguins are able to do this because they are the world's largest penguins – 1 m tall, 40 kg heavy – which is also the reason why they have to do it. Other penguins, as is normal for birds, breed in spring. But something that's going to grow up to be as large as an emperor needs a much longer gestation period. So in order for the chicks to hatch in time for spring and be ready to swim by summer, the emperor penguins have to schedule backwards and start the breeding process in autumn.

When the female emperor lays her single egg in May – late autumn in Antarctica – it has already been gestating for 63 days and there are still about 50 to go. She passes the eggs to her mate then, depleted by all that gestation, heads north to open water for a season of fishing and fattening up. The male holds the egg on the top of his feet and joins the others in a huge huddle for warmth.

SIZE AND ENERGY

Built for the cold

In conditions of almost total darkness, and with winds that reach 145 km/h and temperatures of –50°C, the emperor male incubates its egg. But how does it manage such a feat? For a start, it is warm-blooded and very well insulated. Its size means that it has less surface area in proportion to the volume of its body and therefore less opportunity for its internal heat to escape.

Even with all this, however, the penguin would only be able to survive alone if the temperature stayed above –10°C. The key is the huddle – thousands of males densely packed together. They slowly circulate, shuffling along with their eggs on their feet, so that every bird has to serve its time on the huddle's edge, where it is coldest. Throughout most of the terrible winter any one penguin is snugly inside the mass, where the temperature can reach 20°C.

The penguins do without food during their vigil, but that doesn't necessarily mean they're going hungry. When a male arrives at the breeding ground it is at its annual fattest, and it has the ability to store surplus food in its digestive system, releasing it little by little. By the time the chick hatches, the father still has enough spare food to regurgitate its first meal.

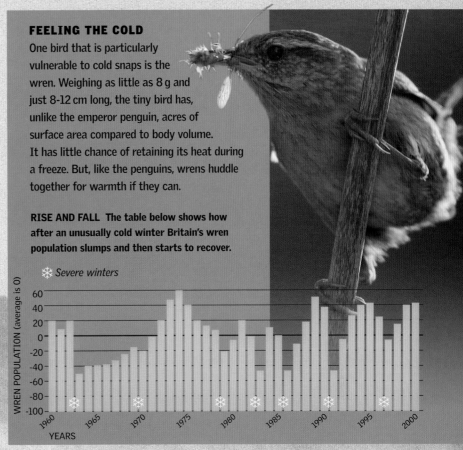

FEELING THE COLD

One bird that is particularly vulnerable to cold snaps is the wren. Weighing as little as 8 g and just 8-12 cm long, the tiny bird has, unlike the emperor penguin, acres of surface area compared to body volume. It has little chance of retaining its heat during a freeze. But, like the penguins, wrens huddle together for warmth if they can.

RISE AND FALL The table below shows how after an unusually cold winter Britain's wren population slumps and then starts to recover.

❄ *Severe winters*

WREN POPULATION (average is 0) — *YEARS* (1960–2000)

KEEPING WARM For insulation, emperor penguins have a thick layer of fat and feathers. There's a layer of feathers, a layer of air and another layer of feathers.

GIANT
PLANTS

A SAGUARO CACTUS TAKES ITS TIME. THIS NATIVE OF THE DESERTS OF SOUTHEASTERN CALIFORNIA, SOUTHERN ARIZONA AND NORTHWESTERN MEXICO can grow to an impressive height – the tallest ever recorded was 17.4 m – but it doesn't get there in a hurry. In fact, most potential saguaros don't get started at all: of the 40 million tiny black seeds a parent saguaro produces in its lifetime, only one in 1000 encounters the right conditions for germination. The rare seed that does take root will, in the course of a year, turn into a plant 6.35 mm tall and after 15 years it will slowly have reached a height of 300 mm.

DESERT NECTAR
In May and June the saguaro cactus produces night-blossoming flowers, which are visited by lesser long-nosed bats. The plum-like fruits that follow are an important food source for many desert animals.

At 50 years old, the saguaro is 2 m and has started to make flowers. At 75, it begins to sprout its first branches, or arms. From now on there's no stopping it: at 100 it is 7.5 m, and at 150 it is more than 15 m and weighs 10 tonnes. After that the plant slows down and lives on to about 175, although some make it to over 200. The oldest saguaro ever identified was more than 300. It was only 12 m tall, but it had 45 arms and weighed 13.6 tonnes.

Root system

Saguaros are the deserts' great reservoirs. Between 75 and 95 per cent of the plant's weight is water. The roots spread out in all directions about as far as the plant is tall, but they don't go much deeper than 15 cm. That doesn't sound like a lot in the way of anchorage, but whenever the roots reach a rock, they wrap around it, giving the cactus some security that way. The root network is very full, and practically all the water that falls as rain – and these deserts do have the occasional deluge – is sucked up into the saguaro and stored between the structural vertical ridges, in folds or pleats that concertina when they fill with water.

UNDERWATER FOREST A diver swims under a canopy of giant kelp in California. The kelp, which can grow as much as 60 cm a day, can rise up as high as 6 m before reaching the surface.

MOUNTAIN EUCALYPTUS

CLASS: Plantae

ORDER: Myrtales

SPECIES: *Eucalyptus regnans*

HABITAT: Grows in tall, open forests in cool areas with heavy rainfall

DISTRIBUTION: Found only in Tasmania and Victoria, Australia

KEY FEATURES: World's tallest hardwood. Can grow more than 1 m a year in order to reach above other trees and and can live for over 400 years

IN 1881, A GIGANTIC AUSTRALIAN MOUNTAIN EUCALYPTUS, OR MOUNTAIN ASH, ENTERED THE RECORD BOOKS AS THE WORLD'S LARGEST TREE. Measured in Victoria, the felled tree was 114.3 m tall. This record was not pipped until 2006, when a California redwood was reliably measured at 115.5 m.

The tallest mountain eucalyptus today is in Tasmania, its height given as 99 m. But some Australians argue that there used to be a lot of eucalyptus trees taller than redwoods. The Ferguson Tree, which fell during a bush fire in Victoria in 1872, was reportedly 133 m, and that was with its crown broken off; it was estimated that, with its crown, the tree would have stood at 152 m. This hasn't been accepted as an official record, but Australians defending the height superiority of the eucalyptus point out that when Europeans began settling Victoria more than 200 years ago there were thousands of huge trees in the forests, and they were cut down without a qualm.

Victoria's old-growth forest is pretty much gone today. The remaining stands of mountain eucalyptus are largely of trees that have grown since the assault began 200 years ago. Since it takes a mountain eucalyptus 400 years to reach its full height, it is argued that some areas of forest need to be entirely protected for 200 more years to allow the trees to grow to their full size.

As for the giant redwoods, their ultimate size has actually been calculated. Taking into account such considerations as the force of gravity, the weight of the wood, depletion of nutrition and water friction, the maximum height that a redwood can grow to is 130 m.

Life support

As a valuable source of water the saguaro is a beacon for all sorts of desert animals. One bird, the gila woodpecker, has found a way to breach the cactus' spines, drilling holes for nesting. So the gila woodpecker – as well as the gilded flicker, which does a similar thing – is the chief builder for other birds, including kestrels, cactus wrens and elf owls. These holes are about 10°C cooler in the daytime summer heat and that much warmer at night and in the winter. Sometimes, even honeybees set up in them. Meanwhile, down at the base various insects and snakes have been doing their own digging and drilling, and up near the top of the saguaro, big birds – red-tailed hawks and Harris hawks – have been building their nests.

The world's current tallest trees – the giant redwoods of northwestern California – also sustain wildlife. The tallest of these, a tree named Hyperion, was last measured at 115.5 m and is still growing. Many of the trees in these forests are more than 2000 years old, and during that time have turned into forests of their own. The taller redwoods make what are known as reiterated trunks, new trees sprouting up from the high, massive branches of the parent tree. One redwood, whose upper reaches were visited by a team of explorers, had 209 reiterated trunks, the largest of which was 40 m tall and 2.6 m in diameter. And because soil builds up on the high branches, bushes and trees of other species were growing there. It was about 30 storeys up but like being on the ground. There were plenty of birds and forest mammals living up there, as well as molluscs and salamanders.

It even happens under the sea. Giant kelp, which grows along the coast of California, is a forest full of animals. All kinds of invertebrates eat the fronds, and living in the masses of branches that act as anchors are sea stars, brittle stars, sponges, anemones and tunicates. Fish shelter in the fronds, and sea otters find their favourite food, abalone, on the kelp forest floor. When sea otters nap, they sometimes wrap themselves up in a kelp frond to keep from drifting away.

Inspiration from nature

Humans have discovered even more ways of using plants than animals. One of the more unusual, though, is to scrutinise a plant and then copy its structure. In the early 19th century, the English gardener Joseph Paxton became fascinated by the giant Amazon water lily, found in the more sluggish parts of rivers in South America. Its leaves are 1 m in diameter, turned up at the edges and very stiff. By placing bags of sand on them, Paxton determined that a leaf could support up to 135 kg.

Although the spectacular plants were becoming fashionable in England around this time, they were very difficult to cultivate. They needed to be under a glass roof that was too wide to be made, according to the glass technology of the time, without breaking. So Paxton set about designing a roof for a lily house based on the pattern of ribbing on the undersides of the giant water lily's leaves, with long strips of metal and narrow strips of glass between them. The design would, on a much larger scale, eventually be used for the Crystal Palace, built to house the Great Exhibition in London in 1851.

GIGANTIC LEAVES A gardener at Kew Gardens in London holds aloft an upturned pad of the giant Amazon water lily.

SIZE: THE DOWNSIDE

LONG NECK, BIG HEART – A GIRAFFE'S HEART WEIGHS 11 KG, TWO PER CENT OF ITS OVERALL BODY WEIGHT. By comparison a human heart weighs 0.45 kg, or 0.5 per cent of its bodyweight. A human neck is about 7 cm long. A giraffe's neck is 2-2.5 m. It's a long way from a giraffe's chest to its head, so its big, heavyweight heart has to pump hard, 170 times a minute, to get blood to travel that far, going almost straight up. So a giraffe's blood pressure is about 2.5 times the blood pressure of any other animal, from a mouse to a whale.

There are, of course, certain advantages to being, at 5.5 m, the world's tallest mammal. The giraffe's height and extremely good eyesight allow it to detect predators at considerable distances. The long skyscraper neck ensures access to a level of vegetation – the upper reaches of acacia trees – out of reach of other animals. And eating the acacia is easy when you're blessed with thorn-proof lips and a prehensile tongue measuring 460 mm long.

Keeping up the pressure

If it needs to, a giraffe can go several days without water, but when it does need to get water at ground level the giraffe has to rely on some pretty elaborate design adjustments. It can lower itself a certain distance by splaying its long legs, and then it can put its head down the rest of the way. But its heart is pumping like an oil well. What happens when the head is suddenly below the heart? What keeps the blood from gushing there? And when it raises its head again, what keeps the blood from gushing back and the giraffe from blacking out?

In the 1960s, a team of scientists set out to answer these questions. They lassoed and darted a few giraffes and implanted

A LONG WAY DOWN A giraffe at a waterhole at Etosha National Park in Namibia spreads its long legs wide in order to take a drink.

instruments and radio transmitters in their necks. One of the things they discovered was that when the giraffe's head is up, the carotid arteries make regular contractions to help squeeze the blood higher, and when the head is down, the arteries swell to absorb the excess blood. At the same time, the jugular vein carrying the blood back to the heart uses a series of valves, like canal locks, to keep the blood from backsliding.

The same mechanics are at work when a giraffe briefly sleeps. It stretches out its hind legs, swivels its head around backwards and rests its jaw on its shank and its chin on the ground. This looks uncomfortable, and a nap seldom lasts more than about 10 minutes.

Why the long neck?

In fact, no matter what it's doing there is something that seems uncomfortable about a giraffe. Why so much neck in proportion to its body, and why so straight up? One scientist studying the dynamics of long necks in general has pointed out that the necks on big herbivorous dinosaurs stretched more forward than up and that height was achieved through limbs and body. The giraffe's nearest relative, the okapi, is also a leaf-browser, but manages to be that without such an extremely distorted body and so many emergency measures to go with it.

Another scientist has argued that the giraffe's long neck has nothing to do with tree-top exclusivity at all, but is a product of sexual selection. Male giraffes fight for the right to reproduce, and they do this by 'necking' – whamming their necks and heads together like gladiators with maces. It's an odd way of fighting. It can be vicious, and necks get broken, but what it means is that the giraffe with the longest, strongest neck is the one that has the offspring. And over countless generations you get an animal that eats tree-tops, not because it has gained exclusive rights to them, but because that is the most comfortable way the giraffe has of eating.

TREES IN THE LINE OF FIRE

To be struck by lightning seems almost a definition of impossibly bad luck. But for the tallest features of a landscape it is a clear and constant danger. Lightning strikes the ground – or the grounded objects closest to electrified clouds – nine million times a day. That's 6200 times a minute, 100 times a second. For the Earth's tallest living things – its tallest trees – that is very bad news, and thousands of trees in populated areas are killed by lightning every year. There are no records kept of the number of trees killed in remote forests. When lightning makes a direct hit on a tree, the sap boils and the tree explodes and burns. Lightning strikes are a common reason for the sudden appearance of a forest clearing.

DIRECT HIT Lightning strikes a tree in the Murganella Nature Reserve in Australia's Northern Territory, transforming it into a giant flaming torch.

SMALL IS BEAUTI

FUL4

LIKE A SPECKLED GREEN PLANET RISING OVER AN ALIEN HORIZON, an alga called *Volvox* steers its way upwards from the bottom of a pond. *Volvox* is smaller than a pinhead, but this tiny organism is surprisingly sophisticated. It has hundreds of cells set in a delicate sphere of jelly, each cell equipped with a pair of microscopic hairs and a sensor for detecting light. Shortly after dawn, the cells react to the strengthening light, and the hairs start to beat, propelling the sphere towards the sunlit surface. Why does this happen? Because *Volvox* has an appointment to keep. Like all algae, it needs sunlight to grow. It is a perfect demonstration of one of nature's rules, affirmed by some of the world's most widespread life forms, from microscopic single-celled protists to insects to rodents: you don't have to be big to be a big success.

SMALL BEGINNINGS

WHEN LIFE FIRST APPEARED ON EARTH, BEING SMALL WAS THE RULE. All living things consisted of single cells, just a few thousandths of a millimetre across. These primeval pioneers were bacteria, and most of them lived in the seas.

Bacteria are still very much with us – in fact, they outnumber all other forms of life put together. And in the living world, nothing can beat them at coping with extremes. Bacteria called thermophiles can survive temperatures above boiling point, while others spend their entire lives in water that is ten times saltier than the sea. One kind, called *Deinococcus radiodurans*, is the most radiation-resistant living thing. It can survive 500 times the radiation dose that would kill a human and shrug off being dropped in acid or kept in a vacuum. It is known as a polyextremophile – something that can cope with extremes of all kinds. With organisms like this among their ranks, bacteria are way out in front in the survival league.

RED WATER Lake Natron in northern Tanzania owes its striking colour to red pigment in photosynthesising cyanobacteria, which thrive in its salt-rich water.

LIVING FOOD Lactococcus *bacteria feed on substances in fresh milk, helping to turn it into cheese.*

Bacterial habitats

Bacteria came into existence more than 3.5 billion years ago, and for most of the time since, they have had the planet to themselves. At first, they got their energy from natural minerals, and many bacteria still do. But about 2 billion years ago, some developed ways of harnessing the energy in light. Known as photosynthesis, this enabled them to spread to many more habitats, from polar snowfields to the shores of tropical seas.

Plants and animals evolved in a world where bacteria were everywhere. For the bacteria, these new neighbours were tempting habitats with lots of food on board. Today, bacteria live on the surface of every plant and animal, and most of them do no harm at all. The average person's skin harbours at least a dozen kinds, and together they keep less welcome microbes at bay. Many plants have bacteria in their roots, where they help their hosts to collect essential nitrogen from the air.

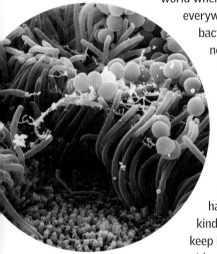
A CLEAN SWEEP Round Staphylococcus *bacteria are swept upwards in the human windpipe by a forest of microscopic hairs.*

But some break through the surface and get inside living tissue, where they can multiply out of control, often releasing toxins – poisonous proteins that can have deadly effects. Bacteria that normally live in the soil produce some of the most lethal toxins. One, *Clostridium perfringens*, causes a condition called gas gangrene, which makes living flesh putrefy. Another, *Clostridium botulinum*, produces a toxin so powerful that 500 g would be enough to kill everyone on Earth. Yet for most of the time, these bacteria live harmlessly beneath our feet.

UNRELIABLE PARTNERS E. coli *bacteria live in huge numbers inside human intestines. Normally harmless, they cause diseases such as meningitis if they get into the wrong parts of the body.*

On the move

Bacteria may be small, but that does not stop them moving from place to place. One of the simplest ways is by gliding – the bacterial equivalent of creeping like a snail. On a smooth surface, the fastest gliders move at about a thousandth of a millimetre a second. At this speed, it would take them half an hour to travel the width of a human hair.

If bacteria could be organised into a race, ones that swim would leave the gliders far behind. These have their own onboard turbines – the only examples of spinning motors in the living world. Set in a bacterium's cell wall, each turbine consists of a tiny collar, with an even smaller rotor inside. Running at full speed, these nanoturbines can rotate at 6000 rpm – equivalent to a car engine running at full throttle. They are connected to long hairs, called flagella, which twist into a spiral shape when turned, making them push like stretched-out propellers.

Until recently, the fastest turbine-powered bacterium was thought to be a kind called *Bdellovibrio*. It lives in freshwater and preys on other bacteria, hurtling towards them at 0.16 mm per second – the equivalent of a cheetah running at 540 km/h. But its place in the record books has been taken by a newly discovered microbe, *Ovobacter propellens*. Using a huge tuft of up to 400 flagella, it speeds through seabed sediment at up to 1 mm a second. Scaled up to the size of a racing car, this extraordinary microbe could complete a circuit of a Formula One track in just 6 seconds.

SINGLE-CELLED LIFE

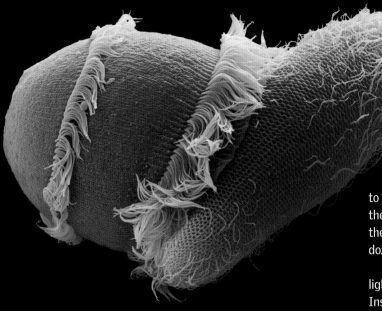

MICROSCOPIC HUNTER *Life is far from safe even for fast movers like* Paramecium *(on the right). Here, its predator is another protozoan,* Didinium, *which paralyses its victim by firing minute poisoned harpoons into it. It then swallows the* Paramecium *whole, stretching like a balloon to stow it away.*

MORE COMPLEX THAN BACTERIA, BUT SIMPLER THAN PLANTS AND ANIMALS, PROTISTS TEEM IN WATERY HABITATS ALL OVER THE WORLD. Seen through a microscope, many are extraordinarily beautiful. But they also include some of the world's smallest and most voracious predators, which feed without teeth or mouths.

Many of these microbes consist of a single cell, a feature that bacteria also share. But there the similarity ends, because protists have much bigger cells than bacteria, containing a range of tiny structures called organelles. Organelles are a cell's work surfaces, manufacturing sites and storage depots, and each kind carries out a specific range of tasks. Bacteria do not have them, but all other living cells do, including our own.

Split personalities

In the 'macro' world we inhabit, it is easy to tell the difference between animals and plants. But in the micro world, protists often behave like a mixture of both. Some, called algae, live like plants, by collecting the energy in sunshine, and most of them drift in freshwater or in the sea. But unlike plants, many algae have intricate cases that look like exquisitely sculpted shells.

Some of the most beautiful cases are the two-part ones made by algae called diatoms, which abound in all the world's seas. There are thousands of different kinds of diatom, and each has a distinctive case. To reproduce, the halves separate, and each one grows a new smaller half to make its case complete. But this way of multiplying has an odd side effect: diatoms keep getting smaller every time they split. To make up for this, they have a pre-

GRAZERS IN THE SEA Antarctica's huge swarms of krill (left) depend on microscopic algae for food. They collect them with their feet.

programmed minimum size. When they reach this point, they stop dividing and grow new cells big enough for the cycle to begin again. When diatoms die, their cases drift down through the water in their billions, like flakes of microscopic snow. Once they have settled on the bottom, they form layers of seabed ooze, dozens of metres deep in some parts of the oceans.

To survive, most algae need little more than water and light. Protozoans, another kind of protist, are more like animals. Instead of living on light, they need food, and they get it by attacking other microbes around them. One of the best-known protozoans is the amoeba – a single cell that moves by changing shape. Its feeding technique is stealthy and simple: it flows round anything edible and engulfs it.

With their shape-changing lifestyle, amoebas are in the slow lane of the protozoan world. Many other protozoans hurtle through the water much faster, using batteries of moving hairs called cilia. One common kind, called *Paramecium*, has more than 3000 of these hairs, which it uses to speed through pools and ponds. It feeds mainly on bacteria, and it finds them at random, zipping through the water like a microscopic dodgem car. This may sound inefficient, but *Paramecium* has one of the most frugal power systems in the world. Running full out, it consumes a 100 000-billionth of the energy used by a 60 W light bulb.

Unanswered questions

Before the invention of the microscope in around 1600, scientists had no idea that the world was so full of small-scale living things. Even today, the microworld is a bewildering place. Protists are particularly puzzling. Scientists classify them in a single biological kingdom, alongside the ones containing animals and plants. But protists are so varied that some experts think they actually belong to many separate kingdoms.

One thing is certain: without bacteria and protists, other forms of life could never have appeared. We depend on these microscopic life-forms to make the world's ecology work. If they did not exist, plants could not grow, and dead remains would never break down. The human race – along with all other animals – would simply not exist.

PRECISION ENGINEERING Magnified over a thousand times, a diatom's silica case looks like a gigantic cartwheel, with dozens of spokes and circles of tiny pores.

MICROSCOPIC ANIMALS

IN 1883, AN AUSTRIAN BIOLOGIST NOTICED SOMETHING STRANGE IN A SEAWATER AQUARIUM. Only just visible to the naked eye, it looked like a tiny translucent pancake, creeping slowly across the glass. By chance, he had discovered *Trichoplax*, the world's simplest animal. Up to 3 mm across and far thinner than a sheet of paper, it has no head or tail, no sense organs and no mouth; it feeds by digesting anything edible that comes within reach. But although *Trichoplax* is simple and small, it is a giant compared with the world's tiniest animals, which are almost a hundred times smaller still. Animals called rotifers, living in freshwater all over the world, hold the absolute record. The smallest rotifer species are just 0.04 mm across, which means that many bacteria dwarf them. A line of more than 250 rotifers would only just reach across the head of a drawing pin.

In the animal kingdom, small doesn't necessarily mean straightforward. Unlike *Trichoplax*, even the smallest rotifer contains hundreds of cells and is equipped with a full range of body systems. It has a crown of beating hairs that draws food towards its mouth, as well as a digestive system, reproductive organs and the rudiments of a brain. What is more, this minute creature and animals like it are not hidden in out-of-the-way places. Instead, enormous numbers of them live wherever there is water and food.

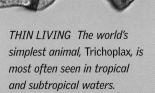

THIN LIVING The world's simplest animal, Trichoplax, *is most often seen in tropical and subtropical waters.*

Creatures called rotifers, living in freshwater, are the world's smallest animals. The tiniest rotifer species are just 0.04 mm across, which means that many bacteria dwarf them. A line of more than 250 rotifers would only just reach across the head of a drawing pin.

Small benefits

Microscopic animals have a huge list of potential enemies. Amoebas can swallow them up, and they are easy prey for a host of other bigger animals. But being small does have some benefits, and these help to explain why nature seems so keen on microscopic animal life.

First and foremost, micro-animals need very little room. Hundreds or even thousands of them can live in spaces that larger animals could not fit into. Microscopic animals called gastrotrichs, for example, spend their lives in submerged sediment, in the minute spaces between individual grains of grit or sand. Micro-animals have micro-appetites, which is a huge advantage when food is hard to find. They are also quick off the mark when it comes to breeding, which enables them to make the most of temporary habitats, such as puddles and shallow ponds.

Many of them have one final trick up their sleeve. If conditions get tough, they shut down their body processes and enter a state of suspended animation – sometimes for many years. Scientists call this ability cryptobiosis, which literally means 'hidden life'. Rotifers are common cryptobionts, but the real experts are tiny creatures called

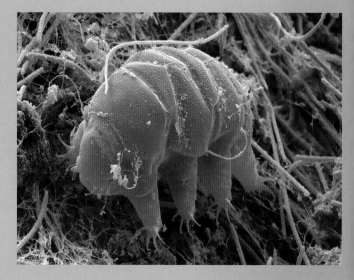

HUMID HOME Tardigrades often live on damp moss, holding on with eight tiny legs that end in multiple claws. If these animals dry out, they can be blown far and wide by the wind.

tardigrades or water bears. Except in the laboratory, few people ever get to see them, but tardigrades are some of the commonest animals in the world. As little as 0.1 mm long, they have cylindrical bodies and eight stumpy legs, and they make their living by eating bacteria or by sucking juices out of plants. Tardigrades live wherever it is moist. If their home starts to dry out, they don't move on. Instead, they launch their emergency survival plan.

When the human body runs short of water, we soon feel the effects. First comes the sensation of thirst, followed by dizziness, headaches and a sense of fatigue. Losing just 5 per cent of your body's water can lead to medical problems. Losing 12 per cent can be fatal. Even drought-adapted mammals, such as camels, cannot survive for long if they lose 40 per cent or more. But amazingly, a tardigrade can lose 99 per cent of its water without any permanent ill effects.

How do they do it? The answer is that they make a sugar called trehalose, which they store inside their cells. When a tardigrade begins to run short of water, its cells start to dehydrate and shrink. At this point, the trehalose turns into a gel, which takes the place of the water and protects the cells from damage. As dehydration continues, the entire animal starts to change shape. Its legs retract, its body shrinks and it turns into a barrel-shaped object called a tun. Once it has fully dried out, all

its life processes shut down, and it looks more like a tiny speck of dust than an animal. Within minutes of a thorough soaking, however, it starts to come back to life.

No one knows how long tardigrades can survive in a cryptobiotic state. In museums, they have been revived accidentally in samples of moss known to have been dried and stored more than a century ago. In nature, where extreme droughts can last longer, they may be able to do even better than this.

FACTS

SEA ANIMALS GOING
THROUGH A MICROSCOPIC LARVAL STAGE
are an important food for fish. These planktonic larvae include vast numbers of young crustaceans, such as barnacles, lobsters, crabs and shrimps. When they start life, the larvae are often less than 1 mm long and can drift hundreds of kilometres before they turn into adults.

LORICIFERANS
ARE MICRO-ANIMALS
that live in sea sediment. First discovered in 1983, they are less than 0.4 mm long and covered with tiny protective plates.

EARTHWORMS'
SMALLEST RELATIVES
live in fresh water and are 0.5 mm long – only just visible to the naked eye.

FACTS

LIVING TOGETHER Rotifers can either live on their own, or in colonies. In this colony, each rotifer is attached by a slender stalk.

SUCCESSFUL INSECTS

INSECTS ARE STUNNINGLY SUCCESSFUL LIFE FORMS. They make up about half the known animal species on Earth and outnumber people by at least a billion to one. They live in practically every habitat on land; the only place guaranteed to be insect-free is the open sea.

There are many reasons for this success story, but being small comes right at the top of the list. The world's biggest insects – tropical goliath beetles – weigh no more than 100 g, and the majority are less than 1 cm long. Among the very smallest of them all are the parasitic mymarid wasps, which can measure just 0.1 mm from head to tail. These wasps grow up inside other insects' eggs, and the males never venture into the world outside. Nature has shrunk them almost to vanishing point, jettisoning everything except the body parts they need to survive and breed.

Being small enables insects to live in an extraordinary variety of habitats that are off limits to bigger animals. These include the narrow spaces inside leaves, tiny crevices in bark and the elastic 'skin' formed by surface tension on lakes and ponds.

THE START OF ADULT LIFE
After many years of living underground as an immature 'nymph', this cicada is shedding its skin and becoming an adult.

DISCARDED PAST A praying mantis clings to a grassblade as it waits for its new skin to harden. Its old skin dangles beneath it, still held in place by its claws.

Bigger animals fall straight through the water's surface, but insects such as pond skaters are so light they can row across it, using feet tipped with water-repellent hairs.

Insects also find their way into all kinds of places indoors. Thrips or thunderbugs crawl underneath the glass of picture frames, while pharaoh ants frequently get inside computers and other electrical equipment, attracted by the warmth. These tiny ants, just 2 mm long, originally came from the tropics, but they are now a major problem in hospitals and office blocks in many parts of the world.

Life in a portable case

Instead of having bones, an insect lives inside a wrap-around exoskeleton, or body case. The case is similar to a suit of medieval armour, made of hard plates that meet at flexible joints. The largest plates cover an insect's back, while dozens of much smaller ones cover every square millimetre of its body, including its jaws, its antennae and even it eyes.

This kind of skeleton may sound cumbersome, but it makes insects incredibly strong for their size. Ants routinely lift objects that weigh 20 times as much as themselves, while the biggest beetles can support more than 800 times their own weight without their body case cracking and giving way. Body cases also put up with an impressive amount of wear and tear. Mole crickets have extra-thick armour around their heads, letting them tunnel through the stoniest soil, while carpenter bees can excavate nest holes in wooden beams that are hard enough to bend steel nails.

Their body cases also protect insects from attack and help to stop them from drying out. The last is a crucial benefit, because small insects have tiny water reserves. Without their waterproof

cases, they would dry out within a matter of minutes – the fate that awaits most small, soft-bodied animals if they accidentallly get stranded in bright sunshine.

Changing shape

Body cases have one huge drawback, however. Unlike a bony skeleton, they cannot get bigger. To grow, insects have to moult, or shed their existing body case, and grow a larger one in its place. Some of the simplest insects, such as silverfish, moult throughout their adult lives. But with most, evolution has trimmed the number of skin changes to less than a dozen. Each

LIFT OFF A soldier beetle's hard front wings hinge upwards as it launches itself into the air. They act as protective cases for the hind wings.

UP AND AWAY A wasp hoists its caterpillar prey aloft. Wasps are gardeners' friends, helping to keep the numbers of other insects under control.

time the insect sheds it skin, it gets bigger; just as importantly, it also changes shape. In some insects – such as cicadas and grasshoppers – these shape changes are quite small, and the young look like miniature versions of their parents. But with most, the changes are saved up for a final transformation when the insect's 'childhood' comes to an end. The insect seals itself inside a chrysalis or pupa, and once this is in place, its body is broken down and completely reorganised. Caterpillars change into butterflies, grubs into beetles and maggots into flies. Unlike their young, all these adults have wings.

Carried far and wide

Insects are by far the smallest flying animals, but their wings make them astonishingly good at spreading. Some butterflies and moths migrate thousands of kilometres to breed, but even the tiniest fliers – such as thrips and aphids – can get swept almost that far when they are picked up by strong summer winds. These insects are so light that they can be sucked high up into the air, forming immense clouds known as aerial plankton, after the plankton that drifts in the sea. Most die in transit, but for a lucky few, the journey ends a long way off in a suitable habitat full of food. And when that happens, the stage is set for what insects do best: breeding with incredible speed.

BREEDING MACHINES

DURING A SINGLE BREEDING SEASON, A FEMALE APHID COULD THEORETICALLY LEAVE 10^{108} DESCENDANTS – that is, 1 with 108 noughts after it, or more than enough aphids to fill the whole of the Earth. Fortunately, predators step in long before this happens. When conditions are good, however, insects can

still build up to enormous numbers in an amazingly short space of time. It is yet another benefit of being small.

In warm weather, aphids can become parents within five days of themselves starting life – a record even for insects and one of the reasons why aphids can be such damaging pests in fields and gardens. Female aphids can produce a new baby every four hours, so within days each one is surrounded by a growing family, dozens and then hundreds strong. Soon, the young are giving birth, so the numbers grow faster still.

Aphids feed on plant sap, and the young do not have to search far for food. They can spread like wildfire when plants are growing fast with plenty of sugary sap to feed their enormous broods. The good times never last, however. Eventually, their food starts to dwindle, and predators take their toll. Like many fast-breeding insects, aphids' main enemies are other insects. Ladybirds grip them in their jaws and suck them dry, while parasitic insects eat them from inside. Wasps pick out the largest specimens and carry them off to feed to their grubs.

Extreme egg-layers

Growing up quickly is just one way of fuelling a population boom. Another is to have an enormous family. This is the tactic used by ghost moths – dull-coloured moths that scatter their eggs from the air. One female examined in southeastern Australia had laid a total of 29 000 eggs and was still going strong with 15 000 left on board. With a 100 per cent survival rate, she would have had 85 billion 'grandchildren' within the space of just three years. But being scattered from the air is a risky start for any insect egg, and most get eaten before they even have a chance to hatch.

In the insect world, the biggest families – and the highest survival rates – belong to social insects, such as termites, bees, wasps and ants. Unlike aphids or moths, social insects live in permanent family groups, called colonies, ruled over by a dominant female or queen. The queen lays all the colony's eggs, but as soon as they are laid, they are taken away and cared for by workers – non-breeding insects that are also the queen's young. Because the eggs are carefully looked after, almost all of them go on to hatch.

During her three or four-year lifetime, a queen honeybee can lay up to 800 000 eggs. And some queen termites produce vastly more even than this. They can live for more than a decade and lay an astonishing 30 000 eggs a day. Even allowing for slack periods, the lifetime egg production of a queen termite can easily exceed 50 million. It is a remarkably efficient system of breeding, which makes social insects some of the most widespread animals on Earth.

FACTS

THE SHORTEST REPRODUCTIVE

life of any insect is that of the American sand-burrowing mayfly. It takes several months to grow up, but once it has become adult, it mates, lays its eggs and dies in the space of a few minutes.

LOUSE FLIES

do not lay eggs. They keep their young inside their bodies and give birth to as few as six well-developed young.

DESERT MOSQUITOES

breed in temporary pools, so their life cycle has to be fast. Some species hatch, grow up and become breed in less than a week.

FACTS

SIDE BY SIDE

AS A GROUP, INSECTS EAT A HUGE RANGE OF DIFFERENT FOODS, FROM LIVING PLANTS AND ANIMALS TO ALL KINDS OF DEAD REMAINS. This, added to their small size, means that many different species of insect can live side by side. Even in a suburban garden, the number of species can run into many hundreds.

Many live by sucking sap from plants or by chewing their way through roots and stems. Butterflies and bees feed on nectar, while small beetles often feed on leaves and seeds. Moths are also common in gardens, and their caterpillars often have prodigious appetites for their size. Some of the smallest kinds live inside leaves, where they make winding trails as the chew through their food. Each trail widens as the caterpillar grows, and comes to an end where it crawls out to turn into an adult moth.

Then there are the predators, the insects that feed on other insects – some of the most useful for gardeners are lacewings and ladybirds, which eat hundreds of aphids in the course of their lives. Finally, there are the insect world's recycling specialists, which take care of decaying remains. The most numerous are tiny creatures called collembolans, or springtails, which dwell among fallen leaves and in soil. A thousand can live in a patch of ground the size of a footprint, breaking down tiny plant fragments so that the nutrients can be reused.

BED OF ROSES The pink and green bodies of aphids swarm over the young shoots of a rose bush. Late spring and summer are feast-time for aphids. They pierce the succulent shoots with syringe-like mouthparts to feed on the plant's sap.

RODENTS

WELL OVER HALF THE WORLD'S MAMMALS ARE RODENTS.
Compared to other mammals, most rodents are small, and few
have good defences – apart from their wits – against predators. To make up for this,
rodents beat all other mammals in producing young in record time.

The rush to reproduce starts as soon as a female starts ovulating, meaning that
she is ready to breed. Males respond to her scent by going into amatory overdrive –
male gerbils may mate up to 200 times in a single day. Once the female has mated, her
gestation period is usually extremely short. A house mouse gives birth in just 19 days
and can produce more than 12 families a year. With breeding skills like these, mice –
and many other rodents besides – can easily produce between 60 and 70 young a year.
If times get hard, female rodents use this abundance in a gruesome way – they cut
their losses by eating their own newborn young.

*GRASSY SHELTER A bank vole watches over
its young in a nest of leaves and grass. Bank
voles can produce up to five litters in a year.*

Lemming plagues

In normal times, predators keep rodents
under control. But if conditions are
good and there is plenty of food, the
brakes come off and a population boom
gets underway. For the Norway
lemming, living in the tundra of
northern Scandinavia and northwestern Russia, these booms happen in
regular cycles every three or four years.

A typical Norway lemming
boom year starts when unusually large
numbers of young lemmings survive the
winter. Soon, they start to breed, and
female lemmings are even faster off the
mark than house mice. Capable of
becoming pregnant at the age of just
two weeks, they can have a litter every
21 days during the height of the
summer. Like a car with a jammed
accelerator pedal, the lemming population growth speeds out of control. After two or
three generations have passed, literally millions of young have been born, which are
then forced to migrate in an increasingly urgent search for space and food. Few of
them find it, and within months the great lemming explosion is followed by the
inevitable crash. By the time winter arrives, most of the migrating lemmings are dead.

It is now the turn of their predators, which in Scandinavia include stoats, to
suffer. Deprived of their lemming diet, their own populations are dragged down.
And this is how the seeds of the next boom are sown. Most prey animals and their
predators evolve an equilibrium, but lemmings and their predators never manage this
long-term balancing trick. With predator numbers at rock bottom, the surviving
lemmings have free run of the tundra. Their population starts to grow again, more
rapidly than that of the predators because they breed faster. The cycle of boom and
bust begins once more.

Mouse and rat plagues

According to one of Europe's most famous legends, a great plague of rats struck the German town of Hamelin in 1284. After all other control methods had failed, the Pied Piper successfully lured the rats away. When his fee went unpaid, however, he returned and piped away the town's children as well. The Pied Piper may have been a mythical character, but rodent plagues are very real. They have caused famine and hardship since the very beginning of farming, and they still occur today.

Few parts of the world suffer as badly as Australia, which originally had no rodents. Rats and mice arrived with Europeans, and these adaptable animals wasted no time in taking up life in the wild. Their new home had few effective predators and, better still, Europeans soon started clearing away the natural vegetation, replacing it with cereal fields – ideal for the rodents. For mice particularly, Australia became the perfect place to raise a family.

The first serious Australian mouse plague happened in Queensland's grain-growing belt in 1917. Since then, cereal farming has expanded, and mouse plagues continue to make headlines. One of the worst in recent years occurred in south-east Australia in 1993. Video footage shows farmers opening the doors of grain stores to be confronted by a sea of mice, hopping over each other as if they were being brought to the boil. When approached, the mice rushed for the nearest wall, rising up it like a wave as they scrambled to escape. All kinds of control methods were tried, including traps and strychnine bait. In desperation, some farmers even used home-made flamethrowers, but nothing seemed to stem the tide.

Eventually, like all rodent plagues, the 1993 outbreak collapsed as suddenly as it had begun. But the incredible breeding power of these small rodents remains a powerful threat in Australia's countryside. One rodent expert noticed that the mere smell of caged mice was enough to make some people shudder – a sure sign that they had lived through the worst rodent plague of modern times.

MOTHER'S CARE A female house mouse carries one of her blind and furless new-born infants. On average a mouse has six to eight young in a litter, but some produce litters of 14.

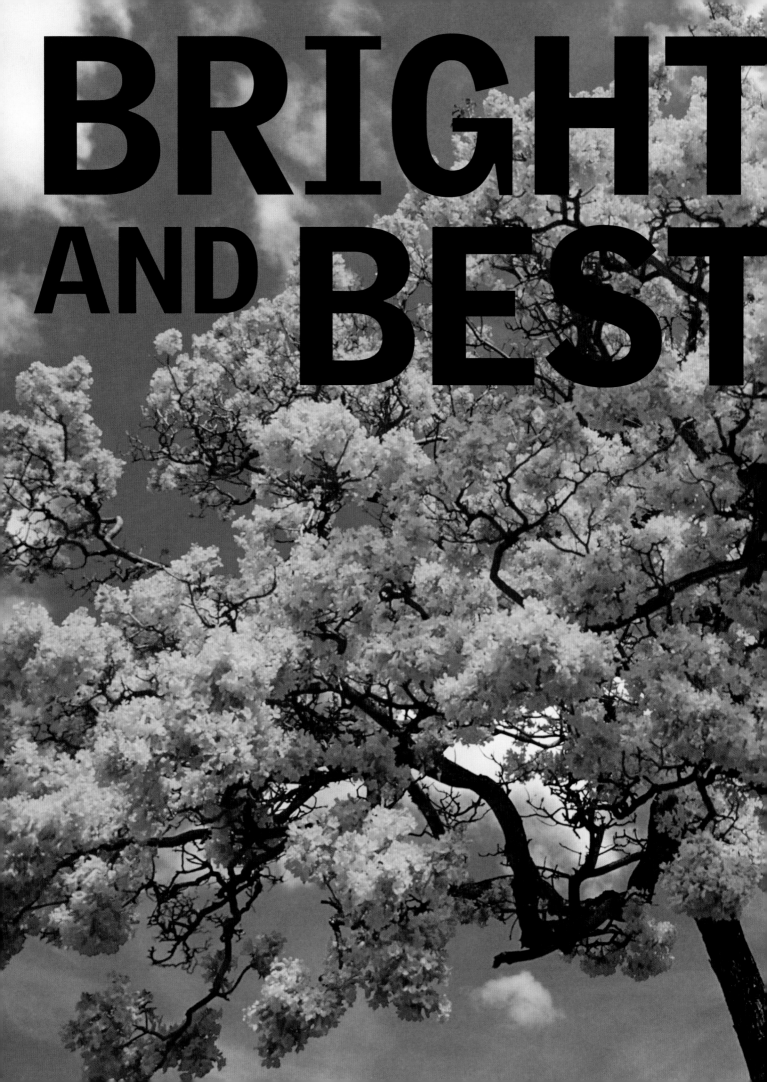

EST 5

THE DAZZLING YELLOW FLOWERS OF A TABEBUIA TREE STAND OUT BRILLIANTLY AGAINST A SPARKLING BLUE SKY. From the intense autumn shades of a Japanese maple to the vibrant pink of a flamingo, nature's palette includes every hue visible to the human eye, as well as colours that only some animals can see. Light drives most of life on Earth, because its energy is used by plants. But plants and animals also use light to create colours that attract attention or warn would-be predators to stay away. Whether they are bold, brash, eye-catching or alarming, they make their colours in different ways, and they often go to extremes to make sure that their message gets across. At the other end of the scale, the natural world includes animals that absorb almost all the light that falls on them. Instead of being colourful, they look jet black.

BASIC BLACK

IN THE LIVING WORLD, NOTHING IS TRULY AND COMPLETELY BLACK. To be like this, an animal or plant would have to absorb all the light that falls on it, letting none of it escape. But many animals come close. Their dark colour comes from a light-absorbing chemical called melanin, which they store in their feathers, fur or skin. Melanin is the most widespread chemical pigment in the living world. It is produced by all kinds of living things, from animals and plants to bacteria. In small amounts, melanin gives living things a golden tinge, but the more melanin they have, the darker they look. As a result, this single pigment can create a whole palette of subdued shades, from the lightest grey to charcoal, and finally to black.

Melanin protects living things from ultraviolet radiation, or UV, which forms part of sunlight. Its short wavelength makes ultraviolet invisible to the human eye, but some animals can see it. Ultraviolet waves are packed with energy – enough to smash apart molecules in living cells, including their DNA. Melanin stops this happening by absorbing the energy safely, like a protective shield. Without it, sunshine would be lethal to many animals in a matter of days or even hours.

BLACK MAGIC Its jet-black fur provides the melanistic cat with good camouflage in the dark forest or jungle and while hunting at night.

Black cats

WELL-SPOTTED Like many big cats, the jaguar normally has black spots, created by melanin in isolated patches of its fur.

It's said that a leopard can't change its spots, but over the generations animal pigments and patterns can change and evolve. Like all big cats, leopards get their black colour from melanin, and melanin production is controlled by genes. Normally, spotted parents produce spotted cubs, but occasionally, a genetic accident – or mutation – intervenes. Instead of producing spots, the mutation triggers melanin production in every hair in a cub's fur. The result is a melanistic leopard, or – as it is often mistakenly called – a black panther.

These striking animals crop up throughout the leopard's range, but they are particularly common in the forests of South-east Asia. When two spotted leopards mate, there is only a tiny chance that they will produce a melanistic cub. But if two melanistic leopards mate, the melanin genes ensure that their entire family is jet black as well. Several other spotted cats have melanistic forms, including the black jaguar from South America, but melanism is very rare in tigers, and almost unknown in lions.

HOW COLOUR WORKS

Sunlight contains all the colours of the rainbow. When light strikes them, living things absorb some of these colours and reflect others, creating the colours that we see.

WHITE SURFACE The polar bear reflects almost all of the light that falls on it, making it look white.

BLACK SURFACE The gorilla absorbs almost all of the light that falls on it, making it look black.

RED SURFACE A cardinal absorbs most colours except for red, giving its plumage a red colour.

Evolution in action

There are examples of black squirrels, black birds, black tortoises and black butterflies, but one melanistic animal famously evolved to match its changing surroundings. Found throughout Europe and northern Asia, the peppered moth normally has black and white wings – a colour scheme that helps to hide it against the bark of trees. Like many moths with dark markings, a genetic mutation occasionally produces a peppered moth with all-black wings.

In the early 1800s, a British insect-collector found a single black peppered moth – something unusual enough for him to note it down. But from the middle of the century onwards, black peppered moths became much more common on the outskirts of England's industrial towns. By the late 1800s, the balance had shifted so much around some cities that the black moth was common, while the 'normal' moth had almost disappeared. Nothing like it had been seen before and naturalists were fascinated.

Before the 1800s, England was largely rural, with few factories and clean air. In these conditions, 'normal' speckled moths were well camouflaged against the lichen-covered bark of trees. But by the mid-1800s, the Industrial Revolution had transformed the landscape. 'Normal' speckled moths now stood out against the smoke-blackened trunks of trees, making it easier for birds to find them. But, with their extra melanin, black peppered moths were better concealed and thrived in the sooty conditions. Then, as cities became cleaner, the balance shifted once again. The 'normal' peppered moths recovered, while the black ones were eaten.

ANIMAL PIGMENTS

There are over 180 000 kinds of butterfly and moth, and no two species have exactly the same pattern of pigments in their scales. Some species even switch between different colours and patterns.

STRANGELY, MANY OF THE BRIGHTEST COLOURS IN THE ANIMAL WORLD ARE NOT MADE BY ANIMALS THEMSELVES. Instead, they get them ready-made from the food that they eat. Flamingos get their distinctive colour from eating pink crustaceans, while many other birds and butterflies get theirs from substances in plants. It even happens in humans. Carotene – the bright orange pigment found in carrots and oranges – is absorbed by the body and used to make vitamin A. But the body only requires so much vitamin A and if you eat three or four large carrots every day, the conversion process stops. Instead, surplus carotene is stored in cells in the skin. If your skin is fair, you will end up with a noticeable yellowy-orange 'glow'.

Few wild animals feed on carrots, but many are coloured by pigments that they get from food. In birds, carotene and pigments like it produce countless shades of red, orange and yellow, and also the flamingo's pink hue. One of the most brilliant of these pigments, called zoonerythrin, gives the northern cardinal its intense scarlet plumage, making it North America's most colourful garden bird.

For birds, plant-based colours can play an important part in breeding and raising a family. Male house finches have bright red or yellow breasts – two colours that come from feeding on seeds that are rich in carotene. The more food a male can find, the brighter its feathers become. As a result, females can see at a glance which males are the healthiest mates. Dull-coloured males are less likely to bring enough food back to the nest.

On the wing

Birds store pigments in their feathers, butterflies store theirs in their scales. Seen under a microscope, these scales look like tiny overlapping tiles, attached by the slenderest of stalks. Each scale has a hard outer surface, separated by a narrow space – the perfect place for pigments to be put on show.

SCALES OF BEAUTY This white nymph butterfly from the Australian tropics gets its colour from chemical pigments stored in its wing scales.

The scales on a butterfly's body are often filled with melanin, giving them a matt black colour that soaks up warmth when a butterfly basks in the sun. Wing scales contain other pigments as well – including some called pterins, which were first discovered in butterflies. Together, these pigments can produce a huge range of colours from creamy yellow to fiery orange and deep sunset red. Butterfly wings often have complex patterns, and each scale works like a single-coloured pixel in the overall display. Some butterflies, called clearwings, have almost no colour at all: when they take their maiden flight, most of their scales fall off, leaving transparent wings held out by a network of dark veins.

There are over 180 000 kinds of butterfly and moth, and no two species have exactly the same pattern of pigments in their scales. Some species even switch between different colours and patterns, depending on the time of year when they emerge from their chrysalis. These insects have so many scales and such a wide range of pigments, the total number of possible patterns is greater than the total number of insects on Earth.

IN THE PINK Wild flamingos are often pinker than ones in zoos, because they get lots of carotene in their food.

Fading away

Like the pigments used by artists, animal pigments also fade over time. A butterfly cannot replace its scales, or top up its colour, so as the weeks go by, the flawless insect that emerged from its chrysalis visibly starts to age. Birds and mammals cannot avoid ageing either, but they do have a way of giving their colour an overhaul. When they moult, they replace their feathers or fur, allowing them to recharge their colour, or even to change it completely.

Birds put on their brightest colours just before they breed, and the transformation can be startling. In winter, puffins are drab so they are difficult to pick out against the greyness of the sea. But in spring, when they come to land to nest, they are strikingly different. Their fresh plumage looks like an impeccable evening suit, contrasting with a multicoloured beak and bright red feet. Some mammals go through an even more dramatic make over. Most Arctic foxes are pure white during the winter, but when spring arrives, they moult their fur and change to a shade of bluish grey. By altering the amount of melanin in their fur, they get the best camouflage all year round.

PIGMENTS AT WORK

IF AN OCTOPUS IS IN DANGER, IT CAN SQUIRT OUT A BILLOWING CLOUD OF DARK-COLOURED INK. While its enemy struggles through this murky smoke screen, the octopus makes a speedy getaway. This disappearing trick is just one example of the way in which animals use chemical colours – or pigments – in strange and surprising ways. Octopus ink contains melanin, the same pigment that produces dark colours in feathers or fur. Octopuses store their ink in an elastic pouch that opens into a forward pointing nozzle. When danger strikes, the octopus points the funnel towards its enemy, and then squeezes the sac so that all its ink is expelled. It's a trick that runs in the family, because the octopus's close relatives – cuttlefish and squid – also use dark-coloured ink to help them escape from trouble.

To dye for
People have known about these natural inks for thousands of years. In ancient Roman times, real ink was prepared by catching cuttlefish and leaving their ink sacs out in the sun. Once they were dry, the sacs were ground into a powder, which was then mixed with shellac, a sticky secretion obtained from sap-sucking bugs. The result was sepia – a dark brown ink used by artists and writers for centuries, and still available today.

FACTS

MOLLUSCS CALLED SEA HARES RELEASE RED OR PURPLE INK IF
threatened. To predators the ink smells like food, so they try to eat it while the sea hare makes its escape.

COCHINEAL WAS PRIZED AS A DYE BY THE AZTECS.
The intense scarlet liquid is made by sap-sucking bugs that live on cacti.

A LOBSTER'S BLOOD CARRIES
oxygen using a pigment called haemocyanin. This contains atoms of copper, which makes a lobster's blood look blue.

FACTS

In the Mediterranean region, a pigment called imperial purple was collected from a sea snail called the dye murex. It was highly prized, because unlike many other colours, this rich purple-red did not fade. In ancient Rome, wearing purple was the prerogative of the emperor and other high-ranking officials, and the methods needed to prepare it were a closely guarded secret. Paradoxically, the dye murex itself does not put its purple on show. The pigment is in the soft parts of the mollusc's body, but is missing from its ordinary-looking light brown shell.

Blue blood, red blood
Lobsters have blue blood, while insect blood is often yellowish green, but in mammals and birds – and in some other animals as

INKY WATERS Startled by a diver, a giant Pacific octopus covers its exit by squirting out a cloud of ink.

HIDDEN PIGMENTS Marine snails often have coloured shells, but some have even brighter pigments inside their bodies.

well – blood is a deep and vivid red. As a colour, its staying power is legendary: years later, traces of blood have been used to solve crimes, and in some cases even change the course of history. Blood stains fade, but they are notoriously difficult to remove.

But why does blood have such a remarkably lurid colour? The answer lies in the pigment haemoglobin, which is present inside red blood cells. Each molecule of haemoglobin contains rings of carbon atoms, with iron atoms at their centre. Called heme groups, these rings absorb yellow, green and blue light, but they strongly reflect particular wavelengths of red light, giving blood its distinctive crimson hue.

A shrew's body contains only about two milligrams of haemoglobin, while a blue whale's can contain three-quarters of a tonne, but in both these animals – and all other ones with backbones – this pigment keeps every single one of the body's cells alive. It does it by collecting oxygen as blood passes through an animal's lungs or gills. Haemoglobin then ferries this oxygen around the body, handing it over to living cells. During this process, haemoglobin molecules change colour. While they are carrying oxygen, they make blood bright red, but after they have given it up, the blood turns darker, until its haemoglobin collects oxygen once more. In small animals, such as shrews, blood circulates so quickly that haemoglobin changes colour hundreds of thousands of times in a day.

Extreme breathers

Like the dye murex's private purple, haemoglobin is usually hidden away. Even when predators make a messy kill, scavengers make sure that every speck of blood is licked up or scraped away. But in habitats where oxygen is short, haemoglobin paints some living animals a distinctive bright blood red. One of these animals is the sludge worm – a small but extremely common animal found all around the world. It lives in the mud at the bottom of ponds and ditches, often in wriggling clumps that look like bright pink hair. Stagnant water is often short of oxygen, but the sludge worm's haemoglobin makes sure that it gets enough to survive.

At the bottom of the Pacific Ocean, giant tubeworms face an even greater struggle in collecting the oxygen they need. They live around volcanic vents, where minerals gushing up from the Earth's crust quickly combine with any oxygen that they meet. To collect their own share of this oxygen, giant tubeworms have a plume of flesh where most worms have a head. Bigger than a human hand, it is coloured deep red by the biggest molecules of haemoglobin in the world.

RED OR DEAD Thanks to their haemoglobin, sludge worms can live in water that would kill many other animals.

A HIDDEN PALETTE

IN 2005, TWO DIFFERENT KINDS OF LICHEN WERE LAUNCHED INTO SPACE. Once they were in orbit, the containers were opened, exposing them to extreme temperatures, a complete vacuum and lethal cosmic rays. After 14 days in space, they returned to Earth – none the worse for wear. Lichens are easy to confuse with plants, but no living plant could stand more than a few minutes in space. Its water would evaporate in seconds, and its cells would be killed by cosmic radiation. Lichens take all this in their stride. Living partnerships between fungi and microscopic algae, they can dry out like a crisp. They are so tough that they grow in some of the most hostile habitats on Earth, including rocks just a few hundred kilometres from the South Pole. These ultra-rugged organisms have a variety of different shapes, but many of them – including the two space travellers – have remarkable colours as well.

The death cap is the most dangerous fungus in the world. Just 0.005 grammes of its toxin is enough to kill an adult human, although slugs eat it without coming to any harm.

Although lichens are small, these colours have attracted people for thousands of years. In different parts of the world, people discovered that water steeped in crushed lichens could be used to make dyes. Lichens can produce a whole palette of colours, from purple to canary yellow and green, but they have one drawback: without a fixative or 'mordant', the colour easily washes away. Fortunately, it didn't take long for a suitable mordant to be found. It was discovered that if dyed wool was soaked in stale human urine, the colour would often last for years.

RED HEADS British soldier lichen (Cladonia cristatella) is commonly found growing on decaying wood or mossy logs. It helps break down old wood and puts nutrients back into the soil.

In partnership

The partners that make up lichens – fungus and algae – live and work in different ways. The fungus forms the lichen's tough outer coat, and anchors it to rock or to bark. The algae live inside the lichen, surrounded by a network of fungal cells. They collect energy from sunlight, and use it for making food. The fungus shares this food, but it also gathers minerals and water, which the algae need. The fungus also produces pigments – the chemicals that give lichens their characteristic colours.

One of the most vivid kinds of lichen, often known as yellow scales, grows on rocks near the seashore, where it survives being lashed by salt-laden spray. Further inland, yellow and orange lichens often live on old brick walls, while grey and lime-green lichens thrive on trees. In marshy ground, and in the Arctic tundra of the far north, one widespread group of lichens have grey or green upright 'trunks' with brilliant scarlet tips. In North America, one of these is known as British soldier lichen, because its colours resemble the uniform worn by British troops in the American War of Independence.

In nature, bright colours nearly always have a purpose, but the extraordinary wealth of lichen colours is harder to explain. Some of their colours seem to be for self-defence. The brightest often contain toxins that keep browsing animals at bay, and coloured pigments may advertise this fact. Pigments also screen out some of the wavelengths in sunlight, which may control the way the algae grow. If true, this would confirm something that many lichen experts believe, but cannot prove: far from being an equal partner, the fungus is more like a jailer, keeping its algae under lock and key.

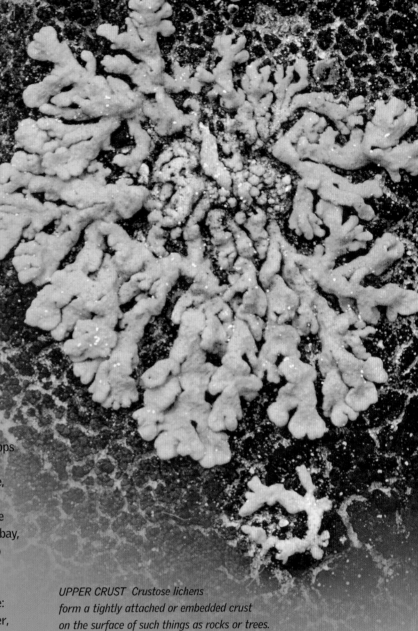

UPPER CRUST Crustose lichens form a tightly attached or embedded crust on the surface of such things as rocks or trees.

A deadly allure

There are over 10 000 kinds of lichen, but far more kinds of fungi grow on their own. For most of their lives, they are hidden away in the soil, or in their food, until the time comes to reproduce. This is when many fungi sprout mushrooms and toadstools, putting some strange and eyecatching colours on show.

One of the best-known fungi, fly agaric, advertises that it is poisonous in an instantly recognisable way. Its mushrooms have brilliant scarlet caps, covered with contrasting creamy-white scales. A well-established favourite in fairy-tale illustrations, it belongs to a family of fungi that is notoriously dangerous. The panther cap looks like the fly agaric, but is brown instead of red. Its toxins are also powerful enough to kill. Strangely, the deadliest members of the agaric family are the least colourful of all. The destroying angel is ivory white, while the death cap is a plain greyish brown. This unremarkable-looking fungus is the most dangerous in the world. Just 0.005 grammes of its toxin is enough to kill an adult human, although slugs eat it without coming to any harm. So why are some fungi brightly coloured while others look dowdy and dull? At present, scientists have no clear answer, but the number one rule for fungus collectors is if in doubt, leave well alone.

Luminous fungi

Some of the eeriest colours in the fungal world can be seen only after dark. As the light fades, some tropical toadstools emit a pale green light from the underside of their caps, casting pools of light on fallen branches, or among dead leaves. Toadstools are not the only fungi that do this. Some kinds that feed on rotting wood give off a feeble glow, called foxfire, which is visible on nights without any moonlight. Toadstools probably glow to attract night-flying insects, which help to spread their spores. But why some fungi light up when they feed is harder to explain. Foxfire has been known about for centuries, but remains a mystery to this day.

THE GREEN PLANET

WATER MAKES OUR PLANET LOOK BLUE, BUT ON LAND, GREEN IS THE COLOUR OF LIFE. It is produced by chlorophyll, a chemical that plants use to capture the energy in light. Thanks to chlorophyll, giant bamboo can grow nearly 1 m a day, while the world's biggest trees weigh over 6000 tonnes. Chlorophyll is found in all the world's green plants. It works like a chemical antenna, collecting energy in sunlight and passing it on to microscopic processing centres inside a leaf's cells. Here, the energy is used to make glucose – a sugar that works as a raw material and, even more importantly, as a fuel. With this energy on tap, plants build all kinds of complicated structures, from giant tree trunks to self-warming flowers that can melt their way up through snow. Energy from chlorophyll is also packed away in roots and in seeds. Most seeds germinate within a few months, but in extreme conditions, some remain dormant for hundreds or even thousands of years, waiting for the right moment to grow.

In a tropical rainforest, green leaves stretch away as far as the eye can see. But much further north and south, autumn brings big changes to many trees. As if sensing the winter ahead, they begin to break down their chlorophyll, so they can stockpile its raw materials, before shedding their leaves. With their chlorophyll fading away, their leaves flare up into bright colours before they finally break off and flutter to the ground.

This beautiful prelude to winter happens because, in addition to chlorophyll, plants have other light-trapping pigments, including bright-orange carotenes and yellow xanthophylls. These pigments absorb wavelengths of light that chlorophyll cannot collect itself, and they pass the energy on so that it can be used. Normally, they are masked by chlorophyll, but once that begins to fade, they briefly make leaves colour up before they too begin to fade.

ALL CHANGE In summer, chlorophyll gives a maple leaf its green colour (top), while in autumn other pigments are revealed to produce a stunning display of colour (right).

Pigments in the sea

Chlorophyll has evolved to work in bright light, but in the sea, seaweeds often use different pigments that are better at working under water. Some of these pigments make seaweeds look brown, while others give them a pink or reddish hue.

One brown seaweed, giant kelp, holds the absolute record as the fastest grower in the world. Unlike most seaweeds, it grows offshore, in water that is often more than 50 m deep. It starts life on seabed rocks as a single cell, but in one growing season, it can develop into a gigantic adult plant that reaches right up to the surface. Giant kelp often grows in large clumps, forming underwater 'forests' that sway gently with the waves.

Red seaweeds contain a pigment that works well where the light is dim, and they normally grow below the low-tide mark, or under shady rocks near the shore. In the 1980s, however, a submersible working off the Bahamas found red seaweed at a record depth of 268 m – deeper than any other form of life that uses light to survive. Light reaching this depth has just 5 millionths of the strength of daylight at the surface. Incredibly, this is enough to keep this deep-water seaweed alive.

LOW-LIGHT LOVERS Red seaweeds contain pigments called phycobilins, which work well when light is faint.

Green animals

The world contains over 400 000 kinds of green plants, but green animals are more unusual. They do exist of course – there are green frogs, green lizards and many species of green insects – but by far the most numerous green creatures live in the sea. Here, many soft-bodied animals swallow microscopic green algae as food. They digest most of the cells, but keep the chloroplasts – the tiny structures that contain chlorophyll and make glucose using light. Somehow they manage to build the chloroplasts into their skin. When these animals crawl or swim into the light, the chloroplasts start to work, and the animal collects the glucose that is produced.

Animals that live this strange way of life – called kleptoplasty, from the Greek 'to steal' – include green sea slugs, green flatworms and even a bizarre green jellyfish, which stores chloroplasts around its mouth and spends its entire life upside down on the seabed, making sure that they get plenty of light.

ATTENTION PLEASE!

IN 1928, A FARMER IN WESTERN AUSTRALIA DISCOVERED ONE OF THE STRANGEST PLANTS IN THE WORLD. It was an orchid – one that grows and flowers entirely underground. The discovery caused a sensation, because most flowers do not hide. Instead, they do everything they can to attract attention. There are over 250 000 kinds of flowering plant on Earth. Some are pollinated by the wind, but most – including orchids – depend on animals to carry their pollen. To attract them, some flowers use scent, but most rely on bright colours. Plants do not use colour at random, because different animals see colour in different ways. Instead, they have evolved exactly the right palette to guide the right visitors towards them.

In temperate regions most wildflowers are yellow, white, blue or purple. Yellow flowers often top the colour chart, from the moment daffodils and dandelions start to open in spring. White is a common colour in early summer, while purple is common in late summer, when thistles are in their prime. There are over 100 kinds of thistle in the northern hemisphere, and the biggest are prickly leaved monsters that tower nearly 4 m high.

All these colours are easily visible to insects, particularly hoverflies, bees and butterflies. Hoverflies are strongly attracted by white, while bees are particularly drawn by short wavelength colours, which include yellows, blues and violets. However, for bees, red and orange flowers are difficult to pick out from a background of green leaves, so they visit other colours first. Butterflies, on the other hand, are particularly attracted by purples, which is why thistles can lure them from far away. So the varied colours of spring and summer are no accident: plants and their insect visitors need them to be this way.

Bird magnets

When European plant-hunters started to explore the tropics, they were amazed by the colours that they found. In 1828, an Austrian botanist discovered the extraordinary flame tree of Madagascar – nearly two centuries later, its incredible show of scarlet flowers still ranks as one of the most dazzling in the world. Even today, botanists continue to discover new species of tropical plants that look as if they have been dipped in pots of brightly coloured paint. From South America to South-east Asia, red and orange flowers are everywhere, and almost all of them are pollinated by birds.

Unlike insects, birds have no difficulty telling the red colour of flowers from the green colour of leaves. Over millions of years, tropical plants have developed red and orange as their call sign, attracting birds to their blooms.

ON THE RIGHT WAVELENGTH
Attracted by the bright yellow colour, a monarch butterfly (top) sips nectar from a sunflower. A rainbow lorikeet (above) is drawn by the bright red colour of eucalyptus flowers.

WELCOME SIGN Like many flowers, these forget-me-nots change colour as they open, showing insects that they contain nectar. The change is caused by a slight rise in acidity, which makes a reddish pigment turn blue.

Compared to insects, birds have big appetites, and they need to eat every day. In the warmth of the tropics, there are always plenty of plants in flower, so birds can feed at flowers all year round. In the Americas, hummingbirds speed from bloom to bloom, hovering in front of them as they feed. In Africa and Asia, iridescent sunbirds probe deep into flowers with their long curved beaks. And in Australia – where more plants are bird-pollinated than anywhere else in the world – parrots and honeyeaters feast at the flowers of bushes and eucalyptus trees.

MIDNIGHT FEAST A Costa Rican hairy-legged nectar bat laps up a meal of nectar from a bromeliad. Its head gets covered with pollen, which it carries from flower to flower.

Creatures of the night

Two different kinds of pollinator come out to visit flowers at night. The first are moths, which sip nectar with their long tubular tongues. Moth-pollinated flowers grow all over the world, and nearly all of them are white or pale yellow – colours that show up well in dim light. In the tropics, bats also visit flowers. Bats cannot see in colour, but they can tell the difference between light and dark, so bat-pollinated flowers are often creamy white, with a powerful smell.

The biggest bat-pollinated plant by far is the African baobab tree. Once a year – usually at the end of the dry season – it produces a huge crop of brilliant white flowers that look like hanging powder puffs topped by petals. The flowers produce an intense smell, and as night falls, the air becomes filled with bats and the sound of their leathery wings.

STRUCTURAL COLOURS

THE MALE MORPHO BUTTERFLY IS ONE OF THE MOST DAZZLING INSECTS IN THE WORLD. Unlike most other butterflies, its shimmering blue is not produced by chemical pigments. Instead, it is created by diffraction – the same process that makes CDs flash with colour when they catch the light. Seen under a microscope, a CD and a morpho's wing have one feature in common: both are covered with parallel ridges arranged at a precise distance apart. In a CD, these ridges are made of plastic, but in a morpho's wing, the ridges are made of protein and they are on the surface of the scales that cover its wings. Each ridge is exactly 0.22 mm from its neighbours – a significant distance, because this is exactly half the wavelength of blue light.

In cloudy weather, a morpho butterfly looks as dull as a fallen leaf. But when the sun comes out, it is instantly transformed into a creature of exquisite beauty. When sunlight falls on its wings, the microscopic ridges split the light into all the colours of the spectrum, and then reflect it back. As the light waves travel outwards, they interact with each other – a process called interference. If two waves are exactly out of step, they cancel each other out when they meet, and their light simply disappears. If two waves are exactly in step, however, they reinforce each other, creating light that is unusually intense. This is what happens with blue light, and it is why a morpho's wings have such an extraordinary iridescent blue sheen.

Hidden gems

In strong sunlight, male morphos are so bright they can be seen from planes, skimming over the forest canopy. But not all animals that have structural colours put them on display. The sea mouse gets its name from its short, stubby shape and its iridescent golden 'fur'. Actually a worm with a short fat body, the sea mouse ploughs through soft sediment in the shallows, where its fur keeps sand and mud out of the water that it uses to breathe. No one knows what advantage – if any – it gets from its metallic golden sheen.

The beautiful iridescent colours of mother of pearl are completely hidden by the live creatures that create it. This substance – known correctly as nacre – is used by many molluscs to line the insides of their shells. Mother of pearl is laid down in very thin layers,

JEWEL OF THE FOREST Male morpho butterflies recognise each other by their colour. They chase away rivals, and will even try to attack blue cloths waved in the air.

and it is these that create the rich milky sheen. In living molluscs, mother of pearl is completely covered by a body layer called the mantle, and it becomes visible only after the animal has died. The only exception is when it is laid down around specks of grit, turning mother of pearl into pearls themselves.

Lasting colours

Despite being hidden away, mother of pearl has two things in common with the scales on a morpho's wings. Unlike pigment colours, its glistening colours do not fade with time. Even if a shell sits on a shelf for years, its inner lining looks as good as new once any dust has been wiped away.

Morpho wings are exactly the same, which is why fragments of them were once popular in jewellery. Over a century after the height of this craze, Victorian morpho brooches still look brilliant blue. However, to see that colour, you need to look from almost directly above. If you move position, the blue colour seems to come and go. The same is true of mother of pearl, although here the colours that you see often seem to change. It's the easiest way to spot what are known as structural colours, and it's an effect that appears throughout the animal world.

Best-dressed birds

Male birds often use colour to catch the female's eye. Most of them do this by pigments, but some of the most dapper species use structural colours, which make them glint in the sunshine as they fly by. In bright light, even crows have a violet metallic sheen, but for sheer shine, few birds can beat hummingbirds, sunbirds and some species of starling. Common starlings have a touch of iridescence, particularly at the start of the breeding season, but some African starlings have such sumptuous plumage that they look as if they have been sprayed with metallic paint, and then buffed to a mirror-like sheen.

As with all structural colours, this astonishing gloss is produced by interference between waves of light. The structures that create the interference are microscopic struts, known as barbules, which give a bird's outer feathers their smooth and streamlined surface. A single feather can have over a million barbules, arranged with mathematical precision on either side of larger struts called barbs. In starlings, the barbules contain microscopic strips of melanin – a pigment that normally makes things look black. But in African starlings, the strips are always an exact distance apart. If the separation is 0.13 mm, the feathers look bluish violet, but if it is 0.19 mm, the result is greenish yellow. As the starling struts about on the ground, its colours come and go according to its angle to the light, almost as if they are controlled by a dimmer switch.

Some of the most dapper bird species use structural colours, which make them glint in the sunshine as they fly by.

TRICK OF THE LIGHT
Perched on a flowerhead, this male sunbird is in the perfect place to show off its vibrant plumage. Its colours come entirely from the microscopic structure of its feathers, rather than from pigments.

SPACE INVADER The ruby-tailed wasp lays its eggs in bees' nests, and has an extra thick body case to protect itself from their stings.

THE GLITTERING INSECT WORLD

INSECTS ARE ALMOST PURPOSE-MADE FOR STRUCTURAL COLOURS, BECAUSE THEIR BODIES ARE COVERED IN A HARD CASE – AN EXOSKELETON. This case is made of chemicals arranged in orderly layers – just what is needed to produce a blaze of iridescent hues. These colours are found in all kinds of insects, from giant beetles to tiny cuckoo wasps.

All colours of the rainbow exist in the insect world, and the species that use structural colours are the most intensely coloured of all. Tropical bees vary from brilliant blue to deep violet bordering on black, while damselflies often have one metallic colour on their head and thorax, and another on their pencil-thin abdomen or 'tail'. Even moths can have iridescent colours: the Madagascan sunset moth is the most spectacular in the world, with sumptuous metallic colours that would put many butterflies to shame. However, butterflies and moths apart, the most impressive structural colours in insects belong to beetles. Each species usually has a single overall colour, but together, they run the entire spectrum, from hump-backed tortoise beetles that look like glistening drops of coloured water, to species like the golden scarab, owner of the most extravagant and lustrous polish in the entire animal kingdom.

Sometimes insects need to show off, and sometimes they need to hide. That's why some insects – including butterflies and moths – use colours that are made in two different ways. Seen in bright sunshine, the purple emperor butterfly is one of Europe's most handsome insects, because the upper surfaces of its wings have a beautiful purple sheen. The undersides are quite different, and are coloured with chemical pigments in many shades of brown. As a result, the butterfly is easy to spot while it flutters among the treetops, but the moment it settles, it seems to vanish against its background of bark and leaves.

When an insect turns into an adult, it usually has the same colours for the rest of its life. Stick insects can sometimes change colour by altering their pigments, but some iridescent insects can change colour by altering the thickness of their body case. The fool's gold beetle, for example, varies the amount of moisture in its wing-cases, which makes their microscopic layers shrink or swell. By doing this, it can be pale gold in the early morning, but reddish copper in the afternoon.

Fade to white

Pure white is a rare colour in the animal world. Most 'white' butterflies are actually off-white, and even polar bears have a distinctly yellowish tinge when seen against Arctic ice. In 2007, however, a beetle was discovered in South-east Asia that is literally as white as snow. Instead of using white pigments, the *Cyphochilus* beetle produces its colour with a covering of ultra-thin scales, which look like microscopic fur. Unlike a morpho butterfly's scales, or a hummingbird's feathers, these scales have a random structure inside. When sunlight falls on them, this randomness means that they scatter all the colours of the light equally, absorbing none at all. As a result, the beetle looks pure white – ideal camouflage for an animal that lives on white fungi on the forest floor.

GOLDEN SCARAB BEETLE

GOLD IS ONE OF THE RAREST COLOURS

IN THE LIVING WORLD. SOME FISH HAVE GOLDEN SCALES, SOME FROGS HAVE GOLD FLECKS IN THEIR EYES, BUT THE GOLDEN SCARAB BEETLE, from Central America, glitters with gold from its head to the tips of its six sharp claws. This spectacular insect measures nearly 3 cm long, and its metallic colour is produced by the unusual construction of its body case. In all insects, the body case is built from a translucent substance called chitin, which looks and feels like flexible plastic. Long molecules of chitin are lined up so that they are parallel, and then laid down in separate layers, each much thinner than a human hair. The 'grain' of the layers points in different directions – just like in a piece of plywood – and this gives the body case its strength. The key to the golden scarab's colour is that the layers are separated by microscopically thin films of air. Each film works like a mirror, and because the films are an exact distance apart, the reflected light waves interfere with each other to produce a brilliant metallic sheen. The golden scarab has several dozen close relatives, with colours ranging from bright green to copper, but all have the same lustre, making them look freshly polished. Their colours may help to deter predators, but they attract insect collectors. Golden scarabs are legally protected, but even so, many are smuggled out of the forest every year to be sold around the world.

CLASS: Insecta
ORDER: Coleoptera
SPECIES: *Chrysina resplendens*
HABITAT: Tropical rainforests, often on mountainsides
DISTRIBUTION: Central America
KEY FEATURE: One of the few all-gold animals. Its colours are produced by microscopic films of air

COLOUR CODING

EVEN FROM THE MOST DISTANT SEATS IN A STADIUM, COLOURS MAKE IT EASY TO TELL TEAMS APART. Many other signals, including flags, uniforms and trademarks, work in just the same way.

But humans weren't the first to use colour coding – in the animal world, it has been at work for millions of years. Animal colours have lots of uses, but one of the most important is as an identity badge. Many of these badges are subtle, but some are so startling that they are impossible to overlook.

For sheer boldness, few creatures can rival the blue-footed booby, a plunge-diving seabird that lives on the Pacific coast of Central and South America. Its large webbed feet are an intense sky blue, making the bird an unforgettable sight. It is one of four closely related species that inhabit an overlapping range. All are similar in shape and overall colour, but their feet are either red, blue, yellow or brown. Thanks to this colour coding, there is no danger whatsoever of a male from one species courting the female of another.

Birds have many other kinds of colour coding. Puffins, for example, not only have bright red feet, but multicoloured beaks which are brightest during the breeding season; afterwards, the colourful outer layers flake away, leaving a much duller beak underneath. Above all, birds recognise their own kind by their plumage: in some species – such as cordon bleu finches from Africa – a tiny patch of red on the cheek is all that separates one species from another. To a human eye, it is a tiny detail, but to finches, it can make two birds as different as chalk and cheese.

Growing up

An intriguing feature of colour coding is that it can change as animals grow up. The young of many mammals – including tapirs, pigs and deer – begin life with spots or stripes, but lose them as they become adult. Spots and stripes work as camouflage, helping the young to hide in the dappled light on

LITTLE ANGEL Swimming in front of its parents, this young emperor angelfish (right) looks as if it belongs to a different species.

FIRST STRIPES A Brazilian tapir nuzzles its calf (below). The youngster's stripes will disappear when it is about eight months old.

the forest floor. But they also do something else: with a single glance, an adult can tell that the animal wearing them is not a threat. This stops strangers treating them as rivals, and also encourages their own parents to keep them under close watch.

In some species, this 'school uniform' helps to keep youngsters out of serious trouble. European robins, for example, are notoriously bad tempered with each other. If an adult male dares to enter another male's territory, the resident instantly attacks the moment it glimpses the intruder's bright red breast. Just the sight of the red colour is enough: robins will attack a tuft of red feathers fastened to a stick. Fortunately for young male robins, this red colour scheme does not develop until they are about three months old. Before that, they are an unprovocative speckled brown.

Divided lives

Robins grow up quickly, but larger birds can take much longer to develop their adult plumage. Young gannets are slaty brown when they leave their nests, making it easy to tell them from adults, which have creamy white bodies and black-tipped wings. For four years, young gannets feed far out at sea, hardly ever coming back to land. During this time, their plumage slowly changes, with their brown feathers gradually being replaced with white ones every time they moult. By their fifth year, all traces of their young plumage have gone. Gleaming white, they head back to the places where they hatched, ready to pair up and breed.

The most extreme age-related colour changes happen in certain kinds of fish. The emperor angelfish, from the coral reefs of the Pacific Ocean, has concentric rings when it is young that change to parallel stripes in the adult. Hundreds of other fish, including wrasses, parrotfish and moray eels, also go through a complete costume change as they grow up. For species that live in shoals, this colour change probably works like the robin's plumage switch, keeping the young out of harm's way. However, unlike birds, many fish don't simply get bigger as they grow older – they also change sex. The ribbon eel, which lives in coral sand, has a three-stage colour coding that marks each step on the way. When it is young it has a black body, changing to bright blue and yellow when it becomes an adult. Initially, it is male, but it eventually changes into female – something announced by its final colour change, when it becomes yellow all over.

IN BLACK AND WHITE (overleaf)
Like human fingerprints, a zebra's stripes are
unique. These zebra are migrating with
wildebeest in Tanzania's Serengeti National Park.

MEASURING LESS THAN 15 CM ACROSS WITH ITS ARMS FULLY SPREAD, the blue-ringed octopus is tiny compared with many of its relatives. But if it is threatened, its beak-like jaws can inject one of the most potent poisons in the animal world. Before it attacks, its body becomes covered with pulsating sky-blue rings. Their message is simple: keep clear. The blue-

VISUAL WARNINGS

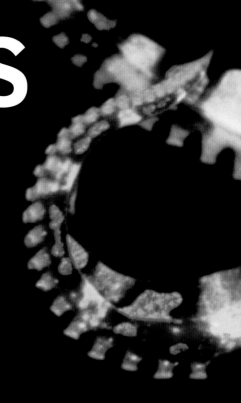

-ringed octopus lives in shallow water around Australia – a habitat that teems with predators. To survive out in the open, it needs good defences, and a way of showing that it is well armed. It hunts by stealth among rocks and coral, and is normally well camouflaged. But if it is threatened – or simply feels that it is – it suddenly darkens and switches on its warning rings.

There is something ominous about this sudden colour change, and most predators prudently back off. However, because the octopus is so small, human swimmers are not always aware that it is there. An accidental brush, without the protection of a wet suit, is all it takes for the octopus to inject its poison-laden saliva into human skin. The saliva contains powerful neurotoxins, which shut down the nerves that control the body's most vital functions. At first, the victim feels dizzy. Within minutes, he or she starts to have difficulty breathing. Without treatment, death can occur within the hour.

With such an armoury, the blue-ringed octopus easily qualifies as one of the most dangerous animals in the world. Surprisingly, though, it was thought to be harmless until the 1950s, and was even kept in home aquaria. But in 1954, a spear fisherman was rushed to hospital in Darwin, suffering from a mysterious paralysis. He died soon after and the trail back to his killer started with the smallest of outward signs, spotted during his autopsy: a tiny puncture mark just below his neck.

Warning signs

When an animal attacks like this, it is actually a sign that something has gone wrong. Because for small animals, warning off a much larger enemy is a safer option than going on the attack. The octopus's blue rings have evolved to do exactly that, and the same defence strategy has evolved countless times

across the whole of the animal world. Among insects, fish, frogs and even mammals, there are animals who advertise the fact that they carry dangerous or even deadly weapons – animals whose firepower is out of all proportion to their size.

For this kind of deterrence to work, it is vital that the message gets across. Here, animals often use a two-pronged approach, the first being to stop and stand their ground. A lionfish, for example, doesn't swim away if it is pursued by a grouper or a shark, and neither does a blue-ringed octopus. Instead, both animals stop and face their enemy head-on. This alone is often enough to make a predator think twice, because animals that stand their ground nearly always have some kind of special defence. If they didn't, they would soon disappear.

The second stage in the stand-off is the visual warning. The lionfish spreads out its fins, which are supported by poison-

DEADLY MENACE With its arms spread wide, a blue-ringed octopus shows off its bright markings to warn predators to keep clear. Its beak is on its underside, where its arms meet.

tipped spines. This makes it look much larger, and shows off its vivid stripes. While the predator looks on, the lionfish seems to hang in the water, as if daring it to attack. On land, skunks have their own tactics. After showing off their black and white markings, some kinds turn their backs on their adversary and do a handstand – a clear signal that they are about to fire a stream of evil-smelling fluid from their anal glands.

Such signals are completely different to any that animals use with their own kind. The reason for this is that signals within species have evolved for private communication. When a peacock fans out its tail, it is an unmissable spectacle, but only the female – or peahen – responds to it by sizing up the male as a potential mate. Female birds from other species are unmoved by the display. Visual warnings are exactly the opposite, because the message has to get across to potential enemies of all kinds. That's why animals pull back when they see the octopus's rings or the cobra's hood. Both signals spell danger, in a visual language that is easy to understand.

If a blue-ringed octopus is threatened – or simply feels that it is – it suddenly darkens and switches on its warning rings.

COLOURS WITH CLOUT The tiny poison-arrow frogs, including the yellow-banded (left) and the granular (inset), make their poisons from substances in their food.

SCHEMING COLOURS

TROPICAL ANIMALS ARE OFTEN BRIGHTLY COLOURED, BUT THE TINY POISON-ARROW FROGS TAKE COLOUR TO ALMOST UNBELIEVABLE EXTREMES. There are over 200 species of these tropical amphibians. They include the most vivid animals on four legs, and the most toxic amphibians on Earth. Unlike most frogs, these poster-painted miniatures make no attempt to hide away. Even in the deep shade of a tropical forest, they are easy to spot as they clamber over logs and leaves on the forest floor. Their self-assurance is well placed, because despite their good looks, these tiny frogs have weapons of mass destruction on board in the form of highly toxic alkaloids – chemicals that are more often found in plants.

One of the most dangerous species, the golden poison-arrow frog, contains enough poison to kill between 200 and 1000 people, despite being less than 5 cm long. In moments of stress – for example, if it is picked up by a predator's jaws – the frog reacts by making the poison ooze out onto the surface of its skin. The merest taste is enough to make most animals drop the prey instantly, but if anything actually swallows the frog, their fate is sealed. For the frog, this is the 'nuclear option' in self-defence. It dies, but so does the predator – the ultimate penalty for ignoring warning colours.

> **One of the most dangerous species, the golden poison-arrow frog, contains enough poison to kill between 200 and 1000 people, despite being less than 5 cm long.**

Warning labels

Poison-arrow frogs have a huge range of colours, including gold, yellow, strawberry and emerald green. Poisonous salamanders are almost as vivid, although their colours are not so diverse. But with all of these animals, colour is only one part of the warning system: just as important is the way it is applied. Some species are a uniform colour, but in most, evolution has turned up the contrast by interspersing the areas of bright pigment with sharp-edged patches or stripes of black. The result is a classic 'aposematic' colour scheme – one that is designed to make an animal stand out.

DANGER AHEAD With its multicoloured bands, the eastern coral snake gives off an unmistakable warning that it is poisonous. It feeds mainly on lizards and other snakes.

In the living world, these high-contrast colour schemes have developed in many different poisonous animals, from bees and wasps to coral snakes. As a result, predators soon learn that anything with these markings is likely to be dangerous.

Colour cheats

Some animals have evolved to become clever mimics of the more dangerous ones. And even with good eyesight and exceptional brainpower, humans are often fooled by these colourful imposters. Some of the most widespread are black and yellow hoverflies, which are dressed up to look like stinging wasps or bees. Hoverflies are completely harmless, and often feed at garden flowers. However, their mimicry is so convincing that many people panic when they come into contact with one.

Wasps and bees are copied by many other harmless insects, including beetles and even some kinds of moth, which not only look like large wasps but can buzz like them, too. Colour cheats are much rarer among vertebrates, but there are some. The scarlet king snake is one of the most convincing mimics of all. This non-venomous snake lives in North America, and it kills its prey – lizards, small rodents and other snakes – by constriction. However, it has an uncanny resemblance to the eastern coral snake, which has a poisonous bite. The two snakes can be distinguished by the sequence of their coloured bands, but to most wild animals, the coral snake and the scarlet king are one and the same.

ERS 6

WE CANNOT KNOW WHAT A STOMATOPOD –
OR MANTIS SHRIMP – SEES, LOOKING
OUT AT THE WORLD THROUGH ITS
EXTRAORDINARY MULTI-FACETED EYES.
Nor can we imagine how it feels to 'see' your
surroundings with your ears – an everyday
experience for many different animals, from
dolphins to bats. Some animals communicate
with sounds that are too deep for us to hear,
and the biggest of them can sense the silent
shock waves that constantly reverberate
through the Earth. Even plants have their own
mysterious senses, which they use to react to
the world around them and to get ahead in the
struggle to survive. Hidden powers like these
have been at work for millions of years, but
scientists are only just beginning to understand
which living things have them, and – more
fascinating still – how they work.

IMAGINE BEING ABLE TO READ THESE WORDS BY STARLIGHT, OR BEING ABLE TO SEE SOMEONE BLINK NEARLY A KILOMETRE AWAY. **For humans, both are impossible, but some animals perform equally amazing feats every day of their lives.** They are animals that have supersight – extraordinary powers of vision that go far beyond the human eye. Vision is an exceptionally complex sense, with many different facets. Strangely, this means that an animal's vision can be better and worse than ours at the same time. But one group of animals score better than we do in almost every area of vision. These top achievers are birds of prey.

Compared to us, birds of prey have extremely high visual acuity, which means that they are very good at discerning the fine details of what they see. Even from high up in the air, they can pick out the slightest signs of movement on the ground far

SUPERSIGHT

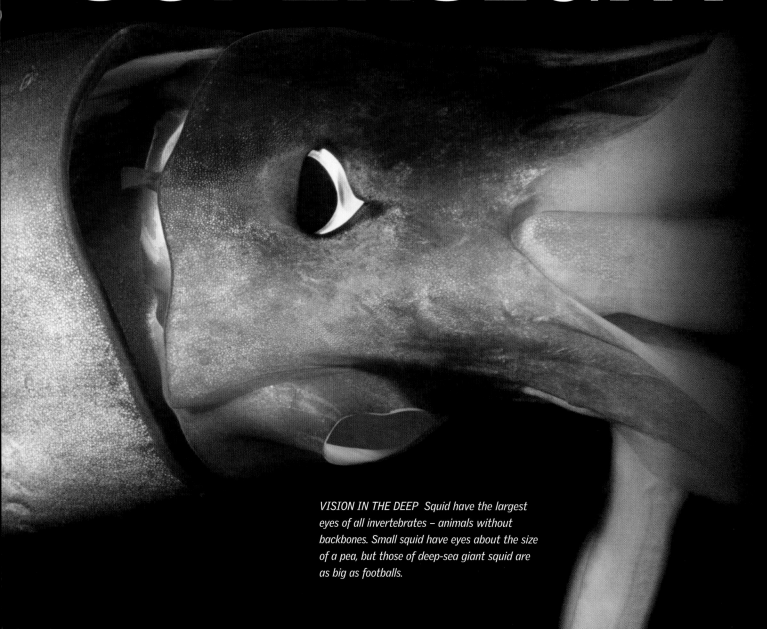

VISION IN THE DEEP Squid have the largest eyes of all invertebrates – animals without backbones. Small squid have eyes about the size of a pea, but those of deep-sea giant squid are as big as footballs.

below. They can do this because their eyes have outstandingly well- developed retinas, the light-sensitive screen at the back of each eye. The retina is packed with nerve endings that sense light, and the more there are, the more detail the eye can detect. In humans, there are about 200 000 nerve endings in each square millimetre of the fovea, the most sensitive part of the retina, right at the centre of what we see. This is far more than in most animals, but there are even more than this in birds of prey. A buzzard's fovea has over 1 million nerve endings per square millimetre – an area equivalent to a single grain of sand. If a human eye were made like this, we would be able to read the small print in a newspaper held up 25 m away. With so much detail coming via its eyes, it is small wonder that over half a buzzard's forebrain is devoted to its sense of sight.

Night hunters

Buzzards are daytime hunters, like most other birds of prey, so their supersight has evolved to work best in bright light. In the evening as the light fades, they settle down to roost. Owls are different, because their eyes have evolved to work best when light levels are low. They cannot see well in colour, but their retinas are lined with nerve endings that can sense the faintest outlines in the dark. This allows them to spot a mouse in one-hundredth of the light that we need, although their ability to see detail is not much better than our own. Thanks to this amazing sensitivity, owls can easily hunt by moonlight, and if the night sky is really clear, they can even hunt by the light of the stars.

FIXED STARE Owls have tubular eyes, which are fixed inside their heads. Instead of moving their eyes to follow their prey, they have to turn their heads. Their necks can swivel up to 180°, enabling them to look directly backwards.

PANORAMIC VIEW Most spiders have four pairs of eyes, which look out in different directions. In this jumping spider, two extra-large eyes face forwards, helping it to judge the distance between it and its prey.

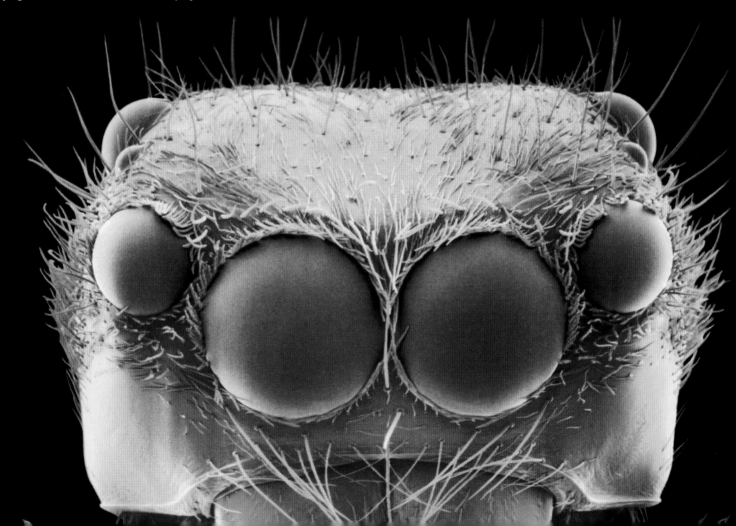

ONE JUMP AHEAD

HAVING KEEN EYES IS ONLY ONE PART OF VISION. JUST AS IMPORTANT IS MAKING SENSE OF WHAT YOU SEE. This process, called visual perception, is something that humans are exceptionally good at, but among animals it includes some bizarre extremes. Praying mantises have superb eyesight, but their visual perception works completely unlike our own. This is because a mantis's brain is focused on one thing only: meal-sized objects that move. If a fly lands near a praying mantis, the mantis immediately gets ready to attack, often twisting its neck – a rare talent among insects – for the best possible view. But if the fly stops moving, the mantis stops as well. Although it can still see the fly, its brain no longer registers it.

This might sound like a major design flaw, but it is very common in animals that hunt by sight. Most frogs and toads react only to moving prey, and the same is true of animals with much bigger brains, such as snakes and cats. Evolution has made their vision work in the most efficient way, by putting most of their processing power into things that move, rather than into a static background. Humans look more at the whole picture, but even so, our eyes also give movement top priority.

At the other end of this spectrum is the common cuckoo. It feeds on hairy caterpillars – the kind that often produce allergic rashes if they touch bare skin. During the daytime, when the cuckoo feeds, most of these caterpillars stay still, and hide on twigs and leaves. But this does not stop the cuckoo finding them, because unlike a praying mantis, its brain stores a 'search image' of its food. If anything matches that image, the cuckoo doesn't wait for it to move. Instead, it immediately snaps it up.

Judging depth

The search-image technique is used by many other animals, including jumping spiders. Instead of making webs, these tiny hunters leap onto their prey like eight-legged gymnasts, sometimes jumping up to 40 times their own body length. Once a jumping spider is in mid-air, it cannot change course. This means it not only has to take aim very carefully, it also has to know exactly how far to leap.

Jumping spiders can do this because they have superb binocular vision, just as we do ourselves. In binocular vision, both eyes look forwards, so that they see the same scene, but from slightly different points of view. By comparing information from both the eyes, the brain creates the impression of depth. This allows a jumping spider to gauge its leap with amazing accuracy. Some kinds even jump off vertical surfaces, such as rocks and walls, to catch insects as they fly past.

For us, binocular vision plays a vital part in everyday life. Without it, even the simplest tasks, such as threading a needle, would be much more difficult. But in the animal world, binocular

PRECISION LEAP Using its forward facing eyes, a Panamanian jumping spider leaps through the air to land on its prey. In case it misses, it lets out a dragline of silk which will catch the spider if it falls.

vision is the exception rather than the rule. Predators often have forward facing eyes, but most other animals have eyes that look sideways, giving them the best possible all-round view.

This all-round vision reaches its greatest extreme in animals such as the hare and the woodcock. Both have eyes that face in opposite directions, placed near the top of their heads. As a result, a hare can see in almost every direction at once without turning its head. A woodcock also has 360° vision, but it has a small area of binocular vision behind it, rather than in front. With eyes like this, it is almost impossible for a predator to creep up on a woodcock by surprise.

Eyes for air and water

Most animal eyes work in air or water, but not in both. The reason is that water refracts or 'bends' light more than air. As a result, the underwater world looks blurred through air-adapted eyes, while the reverse is true of eyes that work in water. For animals that live on or near the surface, seeing can be tricky.

In Central and South America, the four-eyed fish solves this difficulty in a unique and bizarre way. It feeds at the surface of the water, and is the only fish in the world that has eyes divided in two. The top half of each eye looks upwards, and is designed to see in air. The bottom half looks downwards, and has the right shape for seeing in water. The four-eyed fish feeds on flying insects, and it uses its upward-pointing eyes to spot its prey. But while it is feeding, its downward eyes keep a careful lookout for any predators on the move below.

Halfway around the world, in South-east Asia and northern Australia, the archerfish has its own kind of supersight. It is the sharpshooter of the fish world, squirting jets of water into the air to knock insects into its waiting jaws. But because it takes aim from the water, it has to allow for light rays being refracted when they pass through the water's surface. As a result, the archerfish does not aim directly at its prey. Instead, it compensates by aiming to one side. It can fire at insects up to 2 m away, hitting them almost every time. Archerfish develop this extraordinary talent by trial and error as they grow up.

Over two centuries ago, scientists discovered that at either end of the light spectrum, there are hidden 'colours' or wavelengths of light, known as infrared and ultraviolet. We cannot see any of these wavelengths, but many animals can. After dark, warm objects give off infrared light, making them stand out against their cooler background. Rattlesnakes and pythons can sense this light with special organs between their eyes and their mouths. These sensors work like night sights and because there are two of them, like a pair of forward-facing eyes, they allow these snakes to strike accurately in the dark.

An ultraviolet world

For honeybees and birds, ultraviolet is a visible part of daylight, like yellow or green. Many animals have patterns that are only visible in ultraviolet light, while flowers often guide bees towards them by using ultraviolet markings on their petals. But for birds in particular, the 'ultraviolet world' is much more than the world that we see, with an extra colour added. That is because birds' eyes register colour in a much more intricate way than our own.

In a human eye, the retina has three different types of colour sensor, for red, green and blue. When light shines on the retina, these sensors respond to its different colours, allowing our brains to form a full colour image. Birds do even better than this: they have four types of colour sensor. The difference that this makes is almost impossible for us to imagine, but it is as if birds live in a four-dimensional colour world. Things that look dull and drab to us may look richly coloured to them. When a bird sees a rainbow, it may be able to pick out over a dozen different colours, including ones that no human eye has ever seen.

WHAT THE BEE SEES

ALL-SEEING EYES A honeybee's eyes can detect all the colours that we see, as well as ultraviolet light and polarised light coming from the sky. Seen under ultraviolet light (left), many flowers have strongly contrasting markings that are highly visible to bees.

WHAT HUMANS SEE

HEARING

FLYING IN ABSOLUTE DARKNESS, A BAT ZOOMS AFTER A MOTH, TRACKING THE FLEEING INSECT WITH PULSES OF HIGH-PITCHED SOUND. As the bat closes in, its 'radar' speeds up to 200 pulses a second – enough to let it pinpoint its victim and sweep it up in its wings. This extraordinary guidance system, known as echolocation, is used by nearly all the world's insect-eating bats, as well as ones that hunt other kinds of prey. In South America, bulldog bats use it to detect fish near the surface of lakes and slow-flowing rivers, while in Europe, the greater noctule bat even uses it to catch small birds in mid-air.

Echolocation works because these bats have extremely good hearing, allowing them to detect ultrasound – or sound that is too high for human ears to pick up. Humans can hear sounds with a frequency of up to 20 000 Hz, or cycles a second, while dogs can hear sounds at up to 40 000 Hz. Bats can hear up to 100 000 Hz, and they give off bursts at this ultrasonic frequency when they are on the wing. By listening to the echoes that bounce back, a bat can 'see' the world around it, and home in on its prey.

Why ultrasound?

Bats have two good reasons for using ultrasound, rather than the sounds that we can hear. The first is that pulses of high-pitched sound spread out less as they fly through the air. This allows a bat to aim the sound at a target, like a searchlight shining through the dark.

Ultrasound enables bats in the wild to pick out insects that are less than 1 mm across. In captivity, they can fly through the holes in fine plastic netting, not even slowing down as they momentarily close their wings.

HOMING IN With its huge ears facing forwards, a greater long-eared bat homes in on a moth. Each of its ears has an inner flap, called a tragus, which helps the bat to gauge the moth's vertical position.

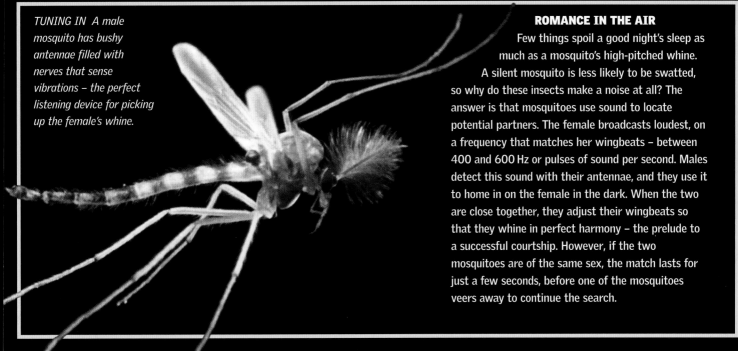

TUNING IN A male mosquito has bushy antennae filled with nerves that sense vibrations – the perfect listening device for picking up the female's whine.

The second advantage of ultrasound is that it gives far more detailed echoes, allowing bats to tell the difference between things that are good to eat, and ones that might be big enough to fight back. In the wild, bats can pick out insects that are less than 1 mm across. In captivity, they can fly through the holes in fine plastic netting, not even slowing down as they momentarily close their wings.

Sound detectives

For echolocation to work, a bat has to be just as good at detecting sound as sending it out. However, the echoes that bounce back from flying insects are often extremely faint. They can be thousands of times weaker than the sounds that the bat makes itself, and every time the distance between bat and prey doubles, the strength of the echoes drops by 75 per cent.

To stop itself drowning out the returning echoes, bats need special ways of keeping the outgoing and incoming sounds apart. Insect-eating bats often have complex folds on their snouts, which direct the outgoing sounds away from their ears. These ears can be almost as long as their bodies, and they swivel like radar dishes to point towards prey. Any echoes that they pick up are channelled towards the bat's eardrums, which pass the sound waves to special sensors in the inner ear. But a bat's eardrums are so sensitive that they need special protection against its own outgoing sounds. They get this from some of the smallest muscles in its body, which brace the eardrum each time the bat makes a pulse of outgoing sound. Using this system, the bat can listen for echoes without deafening itself.

Faced with such effective enemies, moths have evolved their own ways of fighting back. Moths have ears on the sides of their bodies, and many of them can pick up the signals that bats give off as they hunt. Once it has heard a bat approaching, a moth has a few milliseconds to react before the bat picks up its echoes, and launches an attack.

Survival techniques

Most tiger moths often react by folding up their wings and dropping towards the ground. To the bat, it is just as if they have disappeared off the radar screen. But the dogbane tiger moth has a different survival technique: it gives off calls of its own when it hears a bat closing in. This might sound suicidal, but when the bat picks up this sound, it often aborts the attack. At one time, researchers thought that the moth was jamming the bat's signals, but there could be another explanation. Tiger moths often contain distasteful chemicals, which make them an unpleasant catch. By emitting its own ultrasound, the moth might be warning bats to keep away.

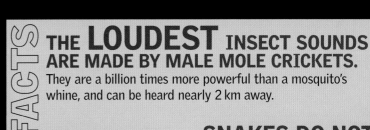

FENNEC FOX

WITH ITS ENORMOUS EARS DOMINATING A SLENDER BODY, THE FENNEC FOX LOOKS FAR TOO DELICATE TO BE AN EFFECTIVE PREDATOR. But this desert-dweller from the Sahara is tougher than it looks, and has been known to kill animals bigger than itself. However, most of the fennec's prey consists of smaller animals, which it locates by its exceptionally sensitive hearing.

Fennec foxes stand about 20 cm high at the shoulder, making them no taller than the average domestic cat. Their ears are up to 15 cm long – bigger in proportion to their body than those of any other fox. The back of each ear flap is covered in short golden-yellow fur, while inside, long silky hairs help to keep out the desert sand. These enormous ear flaps channel sound waves towards the fox's eardrums and to the bones of the middle ear deep inside the animal's skull. In fennec foxes, this part of the ear is specially enlarged, creating an air-filled chamber about the size of a grape. Together the two chambers let sound waves resonate, so that the fox can detect sounds that are far too faint for many other carnivorous mammals to hear.

Fennecs hunt at night, when the air is cool. Using their hearing alone, they pounce with pinpoint precision on beetles and other small animals as they scuttle across the ground. At night, the Sahara can be cold underfoot, while during the day the sand can be burning hot. The soles of a fennec's feet are covered with hair, which protects it against both temperature extremes.

CLASS: Mammalia
ORDER: Carnivora
SPECIES: *Fennecus zerda*
HABITAT: Desert
DISTRIBUTION: North Africa
KEY FEATURES: The world's smallest fox; has the largest ears in relation to its body of any species of the dog and fox family

ACOUSTIC NAVIGATORS

IN THE MURKY WATER OF TROPICAL RIVERS, SOME OF THE WORLD'S RAREST MAMMALS USE THEIR EARS, LIKE BATS, TO 'SEE' THE WORLD AROUND THEM. The largest of these acoustic navigators is the boto, or Amazon river dolphin, a slow-moving pink or grey animal that looks very different from the dolphins that live at sea. The 2.5 m long boto has a bulging head, a long tooth-filled beak, and tiny eyes giving poor vision. River dolphins feed on fish, and they find their food by echolocation.

Echoes from below

In southern Asia, the river dolphins of the Indus and Ganges – which are highly endangered – have such small eyes that they are almost blind. They are the only dolphins that do not have lenses in their eyes. To find food, they swim on their side – usually the right – with their heads nodding across the surface. This strange behaviour allows them to sweep the riverbed with a beam of sound, picking up the echoes of any fish swimming below or hiding in the mud. If the dolphin identifies a promising echo, it takes a breath, closes its blowhole, and dives to catch its prey.

River dolphins have existed for over 20 million years, but their extraordinary way of life is threatened by environmental changes. Noise from ship engines makes it harder for them to hunt, while dams stop them travelling the length of rivers to look for food. The baiji – river dolphins of the Yangtse in China – may even have become extinct. In 2006, scientists who set out to count them along the river found none at all.

A rare ability

In the bird world, steering by sound is extremely rare. In South-east Asia, cave swiftlets use clicking calls to find their way underground, but the real experts in flying blind are oilbirds, which live in the highlands of Venezuela. They are fully nocturnal, and roost and breed deep in caves. They emerge only after night has fallen, flying off in their thousands over the forest in search of their food – the oily fruit of palms and other trees.

Oilbirds' calls have a frequency of about 7000 Hz, which makes them audible to the human ear. The birds also call to each other by screaming and wailing in an eerie and deafening chorus. Somehow, each one manages to pick out its own echolocation calls from all this noise. They use their calls to steer through 500 m or more of narrow winding passages that lead to the cave's mouth. Before dawn, the birds return and the chorus starts again as each bird navigates back to its own nest, deep underground.

UNDERWATER ECHOES The boto's bulging head contains oil that helps to focus beams of ultrasound. Even in clear water it has difficulty seeing objects more than 2 m away.

BEST SMELLERS

Some male moths can detect a single molecule of female sex pheromone drifting on the wind – the equivalent of a drop of water in a thousand full-sized swimming pools.

ODOURS PLAY AN IMPORTANT PART IN THE ANIMAL WORLD. Many animals can detect airborne scent in amazingly low concentrations, and the scents that attract the most are ones that hold out the promise of sex. These sexual scents, or pheromones, are given off by many different animals, but they have a record-breaking attraction in the insect world. To detect a scent, humans often have to take in hundreds of scent molecules with each breath. Landing on the lining of the nose, they trigger sensors that give us the impression of smell. But some male moths can detect a single molecule of female sex pheromone drifting on the wind – the equivalent of a drop of water in a thousand full-sized swimming pools. By steering 'upstream' towards the source of the pheromones, the male moth can track down a female up to 5 km away.

For female insects, scent is the perfect way of attracting attention, because it spreads far and wide. But not all scents are quite what they seem. Over millions of years, many orchids have evolved counterfeit insect scents, which lure male insects to them. Attracted by the scent, a male bee or wasp lands on an orchid flower and tries to mate. While it is busy, the orchid flower clips a package of pollen onto the visitor's body. After several minutes of frustration, the insect gives up and flies off, carrying the pollen with it. Because insects have small brains, the orchid's deception works time and time again, so the insect spreads pollen from plant to plant.

FOOLED AGAIN Lured by the smell, a male wasp tries to mate with an orchid. The orchid's flower not only smells like a female wasp, it has the same shape and texture.

TEMPTING TARGET A John Dory is covered with small parasites, which have fastened themselves to its skin. The parasites do not have eyes – they rely on smell to track down their unfortunate host.

ALL PUFFED UP Alarmed by an intruder, this swallowtail caterpillar has inflated its bright orange scent gland, or osmeterium. This gives off strong-smelling chemicals called terpenes, which keep many predators away.

Smells can also work in self-defence. If a swallowtail caterpillar is touched, it inflates a scent gland that looks like a pair of orange horns. These give off a smell like rotting pineapple – enough to make most predators think twice before turning it into a meal.

Scents beneath the surface

Smell works in water just as well as in the air, and many predators use it to find their food. Starfish follow up the scent of mussels and oysters, while sea anemones sting passing animals when they smell them nearby. Waterborne scents also work as signposts for parasites. Many of these creatures start their lives adrift, but react within seconds if the right host animal comes nearby. Parasites include tiny relatives of shrimps and crabs, and minute freshwater leeches and worms. One of these worms lives in tropical lakes and rivers, and causes the disease bilharzia. It homes in on a single chemical that spreads into the water from human skin.

It is in the dark ocean depths that smell reaches its greatest extremes. Here it is often the only reliable way of finding food on the vast seabed. Some of the best underwater smellers are hagfish – primitive eel-like creatures that feed on dead remains. They can detect the scent of a dead fish or whale over 1 km away. Once they have found the carcass, they look for an opening, then feed from the inside. To keep predators at bay, hagfish pump out slime. Once the danger has passed, the hagfish ties itself in a knot and runs the knot the length of its body to peel away the cocoon of slime – like someone pulling off a sock.

IN BAD ODOUR

THE WORLD'S LARGEST FLOWER, THE RAFFLESIA, ATTRACTS POLLINATING FLIES WITH ITS OVERPOWERING SMELL OF ROTTING MEAT. This is a giant-sized example of one of nature's rules: what smells repulsive to one animal can be exactly the opposite to another. To humans, the smell of rotting meat is a powerful warning sign, but it acts as a lure for flies, because the females often lay their eggs on dead remains. They land inside the rafflesia's bowl-shaped blooms to discover they have been tricked. Instead of laying their eggs, they fly off carrying some of the flower's pollen on their feet.

Noxious nature

The rafflesia flower is not alone in producing this kind of pungent odour. The devil's tongue arum, which is native to the forests of Sumatra, gives off a smell so repulsive it has been known to make people faint. It grows a fleshy flowerhead up to 2.5 m high, which generates its own internal heat. This helps the flower's scent to evaporate, spreading it far and wide. The smell has been described as a mixture of rotting fish and burnt sugar, nauseating to humans, but a magnet for the carrion beetles that pollinate the flower.

Some smells are so extreme that they can act as effective weapons – particularly when they are delivered in a jet that comes flying through the air. In the bird world, young fulmars and petrels specialise in this kind of self-defence. The parents raise their chicks on half-digested fish – a diet that is rich in energy, and also in oils that have a powerful and putrid smell. Young fulmars cannot walk or fly, which puts them at the mercy of predatory birds, such as skuas and gulls. But if anything comes too close, a young fulmar launches a pre-emptive strike. It regurgitates the oils in its stomach, spraying them a metre or more. They can foul a gull's plumage, and cause temporary blindness if they hit the eyes.

Skunks, too, are notorious for their evil-smelling scent, but unlike fulmars, they make their secretions themselves, in glands under their tails. Each species of skunk has its own special 'recipe', but in all of them, sulphur-based chemicals top the list of active ingredients. These chemicals have a characteristic odour of burning rubber and rotten eggs, and the smell is so strong that it lingers for many days. By suddenly squeezing its scent glands, a skunk can fire the foul-smelling mixture as far as 3 m, and it instinctively aims for its attacker's face. The odour is so powerful that it can ward off large animals such as bears and other predators, and even a human nose can pick it up over 2 km downwind.

INSIDE VIEW The rafflesia flower (right) is shaped like a bowl, with a spiky red platform. Its sickening scent attracts pollinating flies.

PROJECTILE VOMIT Aiming at an intruder, a young fulmar chick fires a stream of pungent oily slime. Adults use the same kind of defence to keep predators away from the nests – even their plumage has a powerful smell.

SCARE TACTIC Skunks give plenty of warning before discharging their foul-smelling scent. This spotted skunk's handstand tells its enemy that it has seconds to make a getaway.

TOUCH

PULLING ITSELF ACROSS THE SEABED, A GURNARD FEELS FOR FOOD WITH ITS FINS. The front pair are as dexterous as human fingers, giving the impression that it is crawling with a pair of hands. For animals like the gurnard, touch is even more important than vision in the fight for survival. Its front fins have slender rays packed with sensitive nerve endings, which feel and taste the sediment as the fish crawls past. If its fin rays touch anything edible, the fish uses its bony mouth to scoop up its prey instantly.

Touch works by detecting pressure, often on the smallest imaginable scale. Most mammals can feel the weight of a single insect landing on their fur. The insect makes hairs bend under its weight, and nerves in the skin register this movement, sending a burst of signals to the animal's brain. But the nerves involved in touch quickly get used to what they feel. This is vital, because it stops animals suffering from 'touch overload'.

Deadly vibrations

Insects and spiders live in a world where the tiniest vibrations suggest the chance of a meal. Trapdoor spiders hide in burrows with hinged lids, and rely entirely on touch to sense their prey. If the spider senses vibrations overhead, it throws open the lid and rushes out. One of the fastest species, from North America, takes just 0.03 seconds to make a catch, and is successful nine times out of ten. This is particularly impressive

The biggest tropical spiders, called golden orb weavers, spin webs up to 1 m in diameter, with an extra network of 'guard strands' that alert them when something edible is flying their way.

SEARCHING THE SEABED The gurnard has three highly sensitive rays on each front fin. They constantly tap grains of sand and sediment to find hidden animals.

because the spider is literally in the dark until it opens the trapdoor, and has no exact idea of what and where its prey is.

Web-spinning spiders also sense their prey by touch. For them, webs work like radio antennae, picking up vibrations and channelling them towards their bodies. The biggest tropical spiders, called golden orb weavers, spin webs up to 1 m in diameter, with an extra network of 'guard strands' that alert them when something edible is flying their way.

Radiating ripples

The biggest vibration receivers are the surfaces of ponds and lakes. When flying insects crash-land into the water, their struggles create tiny ripples that spread out through the water's 'skin'. These ripples are picked up by pond skaters – carnivorous bugs that spend all their lives on the surface of the water. They speed towards the source of the ripples, stabbing their victims with their sharp mouthparts, and sucking up their body fluids.

A small number of such insects – called ocean striders – live out at sea. Their sense of touch is so good that they can distinguish the vibrations of creatures from the rise and fall of the waves, allowing them to find food far from land.

FACTS

FISH CAN 'TOUCH' AT A
DISTANCE BY USING SENSORS CALLED A LATERAL LINE. Running along each side of a fish's body, these sensors detect the waves of pressure bouncing off nearby objects and other animals on the move.

MANY WADING BIRDS have beaks with touch-sensitive tips. By probing into water or wet mud, they can catch animals hidden from sight.

EARTHWORMS HAVE GIANT NERVE FIBRES. If a bird touches an earthworm's tail, it reacts in milliseconds.

FACTS

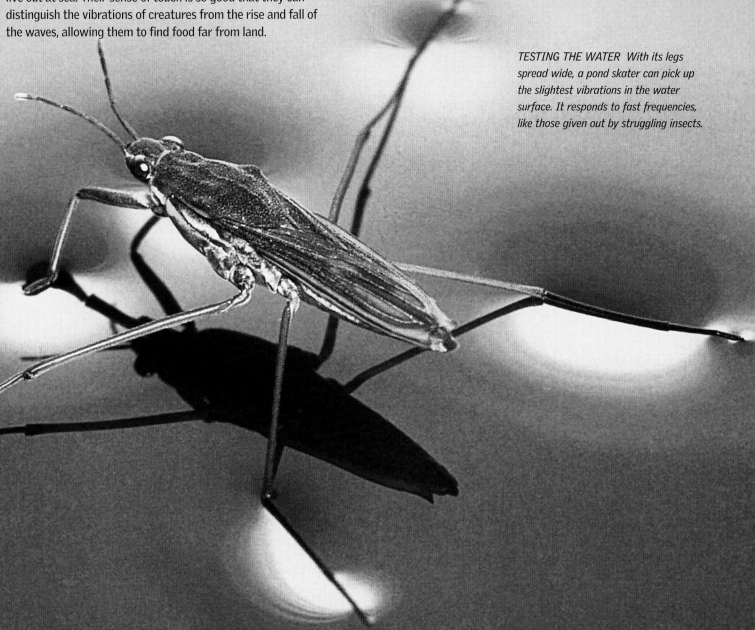

TESTING THE WATER With its legs spread wide, a pond skater can pick up the slightest vibrations in the water surface. It responds to fast frequencies, like those given out by struggling insects.

SECRET SIGNALS

SHORTLY AFTER SUNRISE ON 26 DECEMBER 2004, IN A CAMP IN EASTERN THAILAND, A HERD OF NORMALLY PLACID ELEPHANTS STARTED SCREECHING AND TRUMPETING AS IF IN FEAR. At the time, nobody knew that the animals had sensed the shockwaves of the earthquake that triggered the Boxing Day tsunami. It took two hours for the tsunami to reach Thailand's eastern shores from its epicentre off Sumatra. When it did, thousands of people lost their lives, but all the elephants survived.

Since ancient times, some animals have been credited with a 'sixth sense' that warns them of impending earthquakes. Detailed research revealed little hard evidence to back up such stories. But elephants are an exception: these giant mammals are known to detect sounds – or vibrations – that are beyond the range of humans.

Deep vibrations

These vibrations start where audible sound stops, at a frequency of about 18 Hz – several notes below the lowest piano key. Beyond this is the seemingly silent world of infrasound. The highest kind of infrasound consists of deep rumbles just out of reach of the human ear, while beyond them are frequencies so low that they feel like a physical jolt. For example, a jet engine's lowest frequencies will shake nearby buildings, people and animals.

The bigger an animal, the better it is at picking up these low-frequency waves. Thanks to its large ear bones, an elephant can hear sounds as low as 1 Hz – in other words, a single vibration per second. Sounds like these are made by thunderstorms, tornadoes and distant earthquakes. Because earthquakes unleash so much energy, their infrasound vibrations travel right through the Earth, which means that elephants can pick them up with their feet. Their feet conduct these vibrations from the ground, passing them through the elephant's skeleton to its ears. For elephants, this might well be an everyday experience – one that goes largely unnoticed. But on the day of the Asian tsunami, the vibrations were big enough to frighten the elephants.

Like elephants, whales could work as relay stations, spreading information across entire oceans.

Silent broadcast

Elephants also use deep sounds and vibrations to keep in touch. This remarkable ability was discovered in 1984 by a scientist working at a zoo in Portland, Oregon. Katy Payne became convinced that as well as making audible sounds, the elephants were producing sound that was too deep for her to hear. When the elephants were recorded and sound analysed, her intuition proved to be correct. Beneath their audible snorting and trumpeting, the elephants were 'broadcasting' loud rumbles on frequencies as low as 14 Hz – well below the threshold of human hearing.

In Africa, researchers have recorded these infrasonic rumbles and then played them back, to see how far away elephants pick them up. They were shown to respond even to sounds from battery-powered loudspeakers up to 2 km away. Real elephant rumbles are much louder, which suggests that elephants can probably hear at a distance of 5 km or more. After dark, when the air is cool and still, infrasound travels up to twice as far as it does by day. In theory, this means that a single elephant could 'broadcast' across an area of over 300 km². In places where elephants are still numerous, such as Kenya's Tsavo National Park, these huge animals could form an infrasonic network, with thousands of animals passing on signals unheard by any human ear. Unlike audible sounds, these infrasound rumbles are not muffled by tall grass, or even by trees, but can pass straight through vegetation, making them ideal for communication.

Since the discovery of elephant infrasound, researchers have used recording equipment to investigate sound made by other large land mammals. They have discovered that elephants are not alone in the infrasound world. For centuries, giraffes have been thought of as almost mute, but just as with elephants, the giraffe's world is full of sounds that humans cannot hear. Most giraffe infrasound has the same frequencies as those used by elephants, but one large bull has been recorded producing sound at 11 Hz – the lowest call of any animal on land.

Sounds at this level are too low to be made by an animal's vocal cords, so giraffes must produce them in some other way.

The most likely explanation is that they use their windpipe as a resonance chamber. By throwing its head upwards, a giraffe makes the air in the windpipe vibrate. And because its neck is so long, the sound is extremely low, letting it spread far and wide across the African savannah.

Infrasound in the ocean

Sound travels over four times faster in water than it does in air, and it also spreads further before it finally fades away. This is one reason why the underwater world is full of all kinds of audible clicks and grunts – many of them produced by fish. Ocean sunfish make sounds by grinding their teeth. Croakers make drumming noises with their swimbladders, while toadfish use the same technique to make a startling whistle. Adding to this chorus are the sounds made by dolphins: clicks and buzzes that we can hear, and echolocation signals with a much higher pitch. But just as on land, these calls form part of the acoustic background, because large ocean-going animals also communicate with infrasound.

Infrasound was first picked up at sea in the 1950s by US Navy hydrophones designed to detect Soviet submarines. Beneath the audible sounds of ships and fish, they recorded much deeper sounds that often dipped below the threshold of human hearing. Eventually, it became clear that the sounds were coming from North Atlantic fin whales. Weighing up to 80 tonnes, fin whales are the second largest mammals on Earth after blue whales. They produce powerful pulses of infrasound that last for

ON THE MOVE Infrasound includes all kinds of non-vocal noises. Through vibrations picked up by their feet, elephants may even be able to hear the tramp of distant elephants.

a second or two, adding them together in different sequences that last for 10 minutes or more. The blue whale itself produces even louder calls. Each blue whale pulse has an energy level up to 180 decibels – in other words, 40 times as powerful as a fighter plane taking off. These blasts of infrasound are the loudest sounds known to have been made by living things.

Communication network

Even in today's noise-polluted oceans, the largest whales can probably hear each other's signals thousands of kilometres away. These messages probably work as call signs, telling other whales what sex they are, whether or not they are ready to breed and which species they belong to. But whales have large brains, and they may communicate much more than this. Some of the most useful information might concern the whereabouts and quantity of food. Like elephants, whales could work like relay stations, spreading information across entire oceans. Using infrasound, their communication network could circle the Earth.

ORIENTATION

Birds use not one but several navigation systems – the choice depends on many factors, including the weather, time of day and how far they are from home.

IMAGINE FINDING YOUR WAY HOME WITHOUT ANY SIGNPOSTS OR MAPS, OR ANY OTHER OUTSIDE HELP, FROM A PLACE THAT YOU HAVE NEVER BEEN TO BEFORE. For humans, it would be an almost hopeless task, but it is something that birds do every day. Pigeons have been specially bred for their homing abilities for hundreds of years. But wild birds also show an incredible ability to navigate over unknown terrain.

In 1953, a Manx shearwater was removed from its nest burrow on an island off the coast of Wales. The bird was given a numbered leg ring and flown to Boston, Massachusetts. On arrival, it was taken to the eastern perimeter of Logan airport, and at 8:15 a.m. on 3 June, shearwater no. AX6587 was released. It promptly headed out over the sea and disappeared. On the night of 15 June, on the other side of the Atlantic Ocean, an ornithologist was stunned to find AX6587 back in its burrow. It had flown 5150 km in 12 days, all the way across the featureless sea.

Instinct and experience

Over half a century after this extraordinary experiment, scientists are still trying to unravel the mysteries of bird orientation. To find its way home, a bird has to tell where it is, so that it can decide which way to steer. As it flies, it has to keep on the same course, until it arrives at its destination. As a further complication, that destination is not necessarily the home it left. This is because many of the world's birds breed in one place and spend the winter in another, and the two can be half a world apart.

Some birds migrate entirely on their own, arriving at the right destination the very first time. Strangely, the wild relatives of homing pigeons do not migrate, so they rarely need to use their extraordinary powers. But research with tame homing pigeons has revealed an enormous amount about how birds find their way. Birds use not one but several navigation systems – the choice depends on many factors, including the weather, time of day and how far they are from home. When birds are near home, they use familiar landmarks to find their nests. But when they are in unknown territory, other systems take over. In migratory birds, one of these is an instinct to fly in a particular direction. For example, starlings in northern Europe often fly westwards in autumn to spend the winter in the British Isles.

Starling study

An ornithologist in the Netherlands once caught thousands of these migrating starlings, ringed them and then separated them into young birds and adults. He then had them flown up to 750 km further south, where they were released. When the starlings took off, the young birds headed west – even though this meant they were heading far off course. However, the older birds behaved

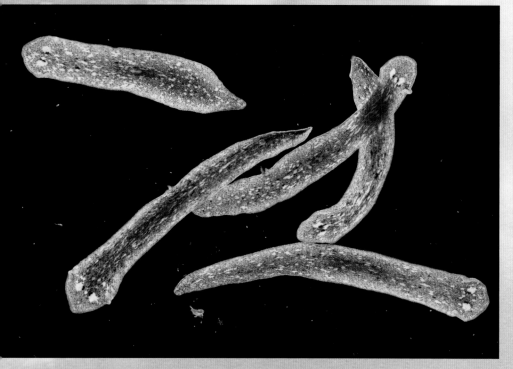

ONBOARD COMPASS Flatworms have very simple nervous systems, but they can sense the Earth's magnetic field. If a flatworm is picked up and moved a short distance, its magnetic sense helps to guide it back to familiar surroundings.

quite differently. They were able to correct their flight path, so that they ended up at the right destination. The experiment showed that orientation is partly instinctive, but also partly a skill that birds learn.

Bird positioning systems

Scientists know for certain that birds can use the Sun and the stars as guides, and that they can allow for the fact that they move across the sky. But the trickiest part of true navigation is knowing where you are. For this, birds must have their own version of a satellite positioning system – one that picks up signals or variations that they can detect, but we cannot. After years of research, scientists have come up with two quite different theories about how such a system works. One involves magnetism, the other a bird's sense of smell.

Humans cannot sense magnetism, although we are surrounded by magnetic fields. These are created by everything that runs on electricity, and also – on a vastly bigger scale – by the Earth itself. The Earth's iron core works like a gigantic magnet, creating a field that surrounds the planet and that spreads far out into space. At every point on the Earth's surface, the field has a particular direction and strength. If birds can sense this, they could tell where they are, and investigations suggest that they can.

In some parts of the world, such as Norberg in southern Sweden, huge deposits of iron create a 'magnetic anomaly', distorting the Earth's magnetic field. For several decades, scientists have reported that migrating birds seem to lose their sense of direction in these areas. Homing pigeons also wander off course if they have tiny magnets fitted to their heads, or if their lofts are exposed to artificial magnetic fields. How this magnetic sense works is unknown, but it seems to involve the bird's eyes, and tiny crystals of the mineral magnetite, stored in nerves in its head.

A nose for detail

Most birds have a poor sense of smell. That explains why many scientists are sceptical about the idea that birds can 'smell' their way home. But in the last few years, evidence has been growing that smell plays a part in bird navigation. Pigeons eventually find their way back home if they are wearing magnets, or even frosted glasses, but if their sense of smell is temporarily inactivated, they get completely lost.

In 2006, tests with homing pigeons in Italy seemed to prove that it is their sense of smell that guides them back to their lofts. However, this is unlikely to be the last word. The world of bird navigation is full of surprises. We still have a lot to learn about how birds manage their incredible journeys so successfully.

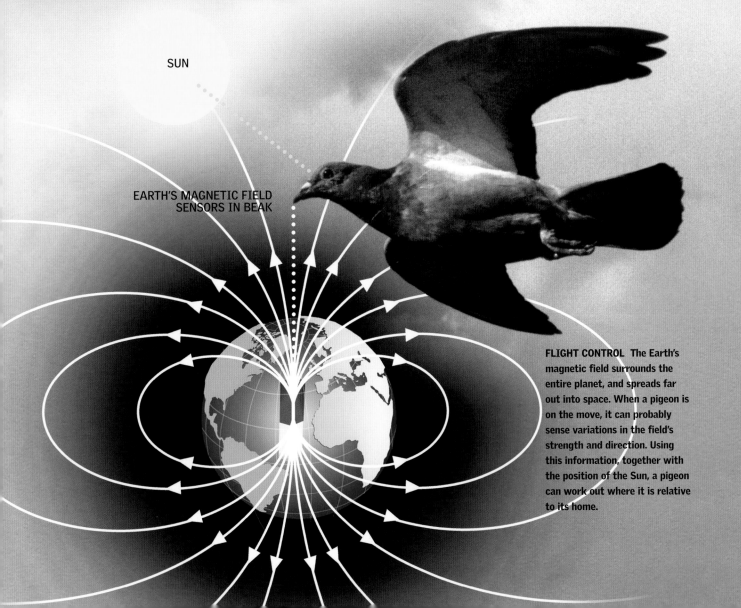

SUN

EARTH'S MAGNETIC FIELD
SENSORS IN BEAK

FLIGHT CONTROL The Earth's magnetic field surrounds the entire planet, and spreads far out into space. When a pigeon is on the move, it can probably sense variations in the field's strength and direction. Using this information, together with the position of the Sun, a pigeon can work out where it is relative to its home.

PLANT SENSES

PLANTS FEEL THE WORLD AROUND THEM USING THEIR OWN SPECIAL SENSES. **They respond to light, to gravity and even to touch.** Some use touch to twine around their neighbours, but others use it to strangle them to death. Plants have their own ways of feeling things around them. Many climbing plants grow tendrils, which look like green tentacles reaching out into the air. If a tendril touches another plant's stem, it starts to wrap around it. In minutes, the tip of the tendril starts to curve, and within an hour, it wraps around the stem several times, getting a tight grip. The rest of the tendril then tightens up like a spring, giving the climber the support that it needs. Tendrils are amazingly sensitive: even rubbing them with a pencil is enough to make them react.

Lightning reactions

Some plants are even more 'touchy' than this. A common tropical weed, called the sensitive plant, has feathery leaves that fold up if they are touched. It reacts in seconds, helping it to avoid being eaten by grazing mammals. The Venus flytrap is even faster off the mark. This well-known carnivore catches flies using leaves that snap shut like two halves of an open book. Its reaction time is one of the shortest of all plants – it takes one-tenth of a second for one of its leaves to close, trapping an insect inside.

Touchy-feely

Plants don't have nervous systems, so they cannot feel in the same way that animals do. Instead, their reactions work by growing in particular ways. When a tendril touches something solid, the cells on the inside of the tendril shrink. Meanwhile, the ones on the outside grow extra-fast, and this makes the tendril bend. Tendrils can even 'remember' being touched. If a plant is kept in the dark for several days, its tendrils stop working because they run out of energy. But if its tendrils are

SPRING LOADED Once they have a good grip, tendrils coil up like springs. This gives climbing plants flexible support, allowing them to bend as necessary.

touched, they don't forget it, and they start curling up when the plant is in daylight once more.

Climbers and stranglers depend on touch for support, but plants the world over need to be able to sense light to survive. They turn their leaves towards the Sun, and some follow it with their flowers. This sense works in a similar way to touch, but light is the trigger that makes their cells grow. Plants are so good at finding light that they can grow up through the smallest crevices between fallen rocks or logs. Planted in a pot, some will even find their way out of a small hole if they have been covered by a cardboard box.

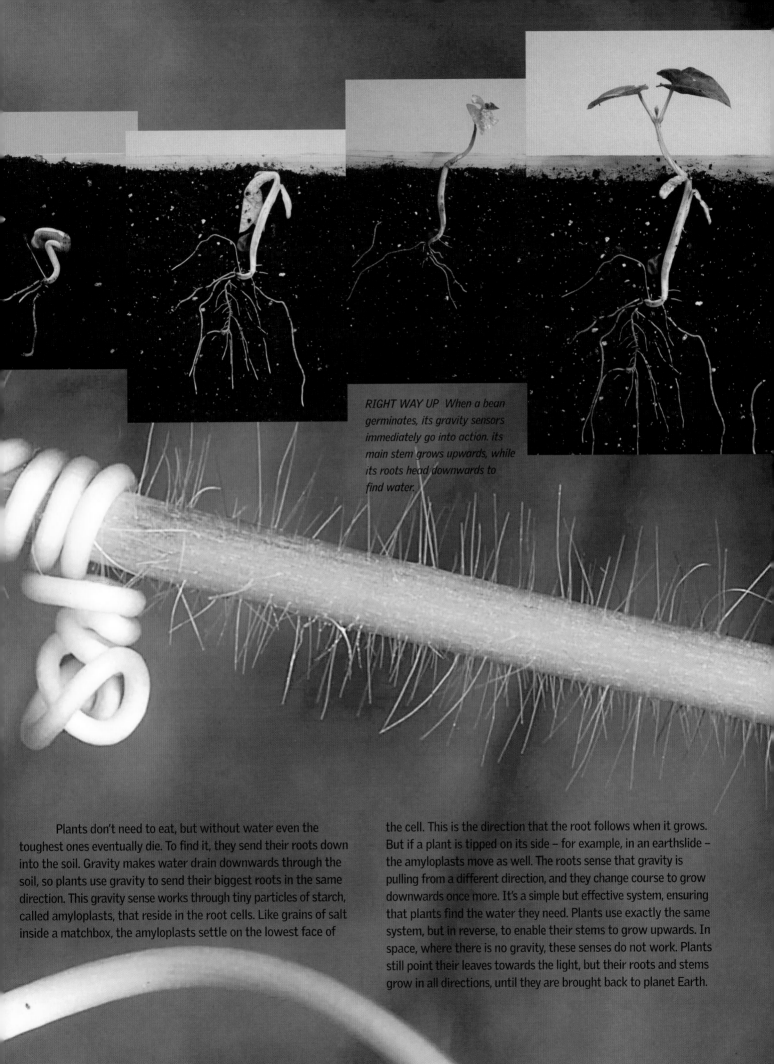

RIGHT WAY UP When a bean germinates, its gravity sensors immediately go into action. its main stem grows upwards, while its roots head downwards to find water.

Plants don't need to eat, but without water even the toughest ones eventually die. To find it, they send their roots down into the soil. Gravity makes water drain downwards through the soil, so plants use gravity to send their biggest roots in the same direction. This gravity sense works through tiny particles of starch, called amyloplasts, that reside in the root cells. Like grains of salt inside a matchbox, the amyloplasts settle on the lowest face of the cell. This is the direction that the root follows when it grows. But if a plant is tipped on its side – for example, in an earthslide – the amyloplasts move as well. The roots sense that gravity is pulling from a different direction, and they change course to grow downwards once more. It's a simple but effective system, ensuring that plants find the water they need. Plants use exactly the same system, but in reverse, to enable their stems to grow upwards. In space, where there is no gravity, these senses do not work. Plants still point their leaves towards the light, but their roots and stems grow in all directions, until they are brought back to planet Earth.

OUTWITTING
ENEMY

THE 7

BACKING UP TO ITS ATTACKER, A SOUTH AMERICAN TOAD PUFFS OUT ITS BODY TO REVEAL TWO LARGE EYE-SPOTS, SET IN A GROTESQUE AND MENACING 'FACE'. Nine times out of ten, this extraordinary piece of play-acting is enough to scare off the enemy. If not, the toad falls back on its final line of defence – a film of poisonous secretions spread across its skin. Throughout nature, the struggle for survival has produced all kinds of escape strategies, some even stranger than this. Predators are often equipped with extreme weapons, so fighting back directly can have fatal results. Instead, many would-be victims rely on bluff, deceit and secret weapons of their own. This deadly game of tactics involves not just animals, but plants as well. It is a contest with just one rule: all is fair in the fight to stay alive.

EXTREME
WEAPONS

FOR MANY ANIMALS, TEETH ARE THE ULTIMATE WEAPONS, BUILT OF THE HARDEST SUBSTANCES EVER MADE BY LIVING THINGS. While mammmals have a set number of teeth, often lasting over 60 years, a shark's teeth are replaced every few weeks. These teeth inch forward as if they were on a conveyor belt, replacing old ones as they fall out. At first, the new teeth are small and flat, but by the time they reach the front of a shark's jaws, they are fully grown, upright and lethally sharp. Teeth like these cannot chew, but they are chillingly efficient at slicing through living flesh. When a shark attacks a large animal, it often starts by biting off a large chunk of its prey. It then circles at a safe distance while its victim bleeds to death.

The world's largest shark – the great white – can have over 2500 teeth at any one time, and the ones at the front of its mouth are up to 7.5 cm long. But because the great white's bite is so powerful, its oldest teeth, on the outside edge of its mouth, sometimes snap off and become lodged in its prey. When this happens, the shark swallows its food along with some of its teeth as well.

OPEN WIDE A European grey wolf shows off its impressive set of teeth (right). These include the long pointed canines at the front, which the wolf uses to grip its prey. Further back, blade-like carnassials work like pairs of scissors to slice up the food.

LETHAL ARMOURY Sawsharks have blade-like snouts that are edged with narrow teeth. Unlike other sharks, they kill their prey with their snouts, rather than their jaws (below).

Cookiecutters and piranhas

No other predatory fish has teeth bigger than the great white's. But even so, smaller fish can be formidably armed. The cigar-shaped cookiecutter shark, which grows up to 50 cm long, bites pieces of flesh out of much larger animals, including whales, while red piranhas use the same technique to attack other fish in fresh water. However, unlike cookiecutters, piranhas sometimes hunt in packs, and they can become highly aggressive when excited by the smell of blood. Despite their murderous reputation, there are very few authenticated records of piranhas killing humans, but with their appetite for flesh, they make short work of people who have drowned.

Multi-purpose tusks

The plant-eating African elephant has the longest teeth of any mammal. These are its tusks – a pair of special incisor teeth that grow out of its upper jaw. Most mammals have flat-edged incisors that they use for biting or gnawing, but an elephant's tusks have an oval cross-section, and they keep growing throughout its life. The tusks of a bull African elephant can be up to 3.5 m long, but in prehistoric times, they were even bigger. One set of mammoth tusks, housed in a museum in the Czech Republic, measure an astounding 5 m from base to tip.

Tusks grow from their roots, at a rate of up to 20 cm a year. However, they also get worn away at their tips, so the overall growth rate is often less than this. Elephants use their tusks in many different ways: they make ideal tools for stripping bark off trees, digging for water or clearing obstacles out of the way. For some of these tasks, both tusks are used, but often only one is needed. Most elephants are either 'left-tusked' or 'right-tusked' – a difference that is often easy to spot, because one of their tusks wears away faster than the other.

When an elephant is threatened, tusks can turn into deadly weapons. Solitary bull elephants are the most dangerous: in the wild, they have been known to kill adult rhinos, and they can tip a vehicle over in seconds. However, after decades of illegal hunting, big tuskers have become very rare. Despite their formidable weapons, elephants have much more to fear from humans than we do from them.

> **The cookiecutter shark bites pieces of flesh out of much larger animals, including whales, while red piranhas use the same technique to attack fish in freshwater.**

JAGGED EDGE Although a piranha's teeth are small and simple, they can cut out several mouthfuls of flesh a minute, enabling shoals of piranhas to reduce large animal bones.

TOOTHLESS WONDERS

ANIMALS WITHOUT BACKBONES DON'T HAVE TEETH, BUT MANY DO HAVE ULTRA-SHARP MOUTHPARTS THAT BITE OR STAB. The biggest of these toothless biters are giant squid – legendary deep-sea predators armed with beak-like jaws. Only one giant squid has ever been captured on camera, but their dead remains are sometimes hauled to the surface in fishing nets, or washed up on the shore. A giant squid's beak looks similar to a parrot's, but it can be 20 cm long, with edges as sharp as knives. Squids use their beaks to slice up prey that they catch in their sucker-bearing arms. No one has ever seen a giant squid's beak in action, but they are strong enough to cut through steel, so would have no difficulty slicing through a human arm or leg.

Giant squid are not the only invertebrates with beaks. All other squids have them, and so do their close relatives, the octopuses. A squid's body contains two hard parts: its beak and a large chalky internal float. But octopuses need no float, as they spend most of their lives on the seabed. Their invertebrate bodies are amazingly supple and elastic. If they can get their beak through an opening, the rest of their body can follow.

A taste for blood

In the insect world, some of the most powerful biters are female horseflies – insects of damp, grassy places that feed on blood. Horseflies often fly silently, using their large iridescent eyes to search for likely sources of food. Their favourite victims are large mammals, including horses and deer, but in the tropics they even target rhinos and elephants, despite the thickness of the hides. Having located its target, a horsefly lands stealthily, and immediately gets ready to feed.

Unlike a mosquito, a horsefly's mouthparts do not work like a syringe. Instead, they slice their way through the animal's skin, creating an open wound. It is a lengthy operation, and a painful one for the horsefly's victim. Animals often try to dislodge horseflies, but if this happens, the fly simply circles its victim several times, before sneaking back again to finish its meal. Once the horsefly has had its fill, it disappears to digest its food – the prelude to laying a large batch of eggs.

Drilled to destruction

When a predator attacks, its prey either fights back, or tries to escape. But the oyster drill's prey can do neither. This common marine snail lives in shallow water, and it feeds on other molluscs

SURGICAL STRIKE A horsefly's mouthparts work like a pair of knives. The fly stabs them into its victim's skin, and then moves them from side to side to make the blood flow.

that are fastened to the rock. Apart from oysters themselves, the oyster drill's favourite prey are mussels. These are some of the commonest seashore animals, which means that oyster drills rarely run short of food.

The oyster drill's weapon is a mouthpart called a radula, which has a surface as rough as a file. Using this, it slowly scrapes a tiny hole through its victim's shell. To speed up the process, it produces a weak acid which softens the shell's calcium, making it easier to drill. Even so, it can take the oyster drill up to eight hours to break its way through, making a hole just a few millimetres across. When the hole is complete, the oyster drill slides its 'mouth' through the opening, and injects fluids that digest the oyster or mussel inside its own shell. Once its victim's flesh is soft enough, the oyster drill sucks up its meal.

CLAWS

IN 2007, A ZOOKEEPER IN BUENOS AIRES, ARGENTINA, DIED AFTER BEING ATTACKED BY A GIANT ANTEATER.

A giant anteater feeds on termites, and it uses its claws to break open their nests, which are made of sun-baked clay and can be hard enough to break open even with a hammer.

TREE-DWELLING ANTEATER The southern tamandua from South America uses its strong claws to break into the nests of ants and other insects, which it laps up as quickly as it can with its long, sticky tongue, before the insects' defences kick in. Unlike the giant anteater, its larger relative, the tamandua avoids termites.

Anteaters are not normally aggressive creatures, but if they feel threatened, their huge, powerful claws can become lethal weapons. Unlike bones, most claws are made of keratin – the same substance that gives fingernails and hooves their strength. In fingernails, the keratin grows in a thin, flat layer, which is ideal for protecting sensitive fingertips. But in a claw, the keratin is much thicker, and it is steeply curved from side to side. As a claw lengthens, this shape gives it tremendous strength. Instead of snapping, claws like this can slash, scrape or gouge.

A giant anteater's front feet have three giant claws, each up to 10 cm long. Claws this big have to be treated with care, and the anteater is careful not to blunt them: it walks on its knuckles, with its claws turned up into its palms. It feeds on termites, and it uses its claws to break open their nests, which are made of sun-baked clay and can be hard enough to break open even with a hammer. As the insects swarm to the damaged part to defend the nest, the anteater draws them into its mouth with its long, sticky tongue.

PINCER MOVEMENTS The lobster's crushing claw – seen here on the left – has hard white nodules that help it to crack open shells. The other claw has straight edges that meet like pruning shears.

Birds with killer claws

Eagles and hawks have needle-sharp claws, or talons, which they use to kill their prey. But for flightless giants like the ostrich, claws work more like hooves. The ostrich is the only bird in the world that has just two toes on each foot. The inner toe is by far the biggest, and it has a heavy claw that digs into the ground when the ostrich runs. Like the giant anteater, the ostrich can also use its claws for self-defence. Male ostriches fight by kicking out at their rivals, and adults with young can even chase away leopards and lions. But unless they are cornered, ostriches rarely stand their ground – instead, they run. Thanks to their 'hooves', they are almost as fast as a racehorse and have the top speed of any bird on land: 65 km/h.

The world's second largest bird, the southern cassowary, behaves in a very different way. Unlike the ostrich, it lives alone in the forests of northern Australia and New Guinea, where it feeds on fallen fruit. It has three toes on its feet, and the inner one is armed with a vicious claw up to 12 cm long. It is a formidable weapon, and one that the cassowary does not hesitate to use.

During World War II, American and Australian troops stationed in New Guinea were warned to be on the alert for cassowaries, because operations took them into thick rainforest, where they risked intruding into the birds' territories. Even in today's more peaceful times, cassowary attacks are still reported every year in Australia. Some result in serious human injuries, and occasionally a cassowary kills.

Self-sharpening claws

Whatever tools are made of, they eventually lose their edge. The same thing is true with animals' claws. However, unlike tools, claws can grow – a crucial difference that helps to keep them sharp. A cat's front claws have particularly sharp tips, and cats minimise wear by retracting them into their paws when they are not being used. But from time to time, cats scratch their claws against rough objects, such as wood. This behaviour runs through the entire cat family, from domestic tabbies to tigers.

When a cat does this, the outside edge of each claw flakes off, leaving a sharpened point. Like a fingernail, the claw grows a few millimetres each month, so that the cycle of wear and resharpening continues right through a cat's life. The same is true of all animal claws: they wear down, but they never wear out.

Precision pincers

Take two claws and add a hinge. The result is a pincer – something that can pick up objects with great precision, or crush them in its vice-like grip. In the animal world, some pincers are so small that they can be seen only with a microscope. Sea urchins have special pincers on flexible stalks. Called pedicellaria, these pincers prevent animals and algae from settling on their shell, so that it doesn't become encrusted with barnacles and seaweed. On land, some of the smallest pincers belong to pseudoscorpions – tiny relatives of true scorpions that live among dead leaves and in soil. Pseudoscorpions do not have stings, but each of their pincers has a poison gland at its tip. They use these micro-pincers to catch and kill their microscopic prey, and also to hitch a lift on larger animals, such as spiders and flies.

Real scorpions can be thousands of times bigger than these tiny creatures. The largest kinds have heavily armoured pincers that can grip lizards and even mice, holding them down and eventually crushing them to death. Once the victim is lifeless, the scorpion eats it in extremely small pieces, which it cuts up using two miniature pincers on either side of its mouth. It is a slow process, but scorpions cannot hurry their food because their mouths are just a few millimetres across.

The world's largest pincers belong to lobsters and deep-sea spider crabs. Reinforced with chalky minerals, they can be longer than a human arm. When a lobster is young, its two pincers are the same size, but as it grows up, they develop different shapes. One pincer has straight jaws, which the lobster uses for slicing through its food. The other one is often larger, with crooked jaws that are good at gripping and crushing shells. Using this, a large lobster can exert 30 times as much force as a nutcracker, smashing its prey apart.

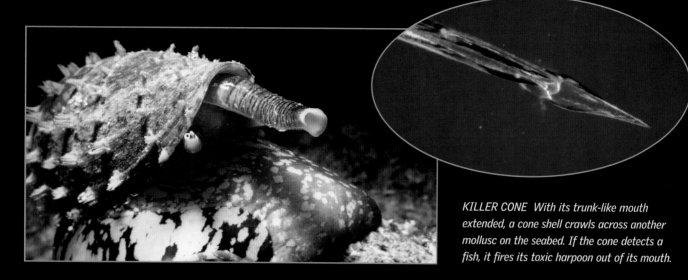

KILLER CONE With its trunk-like mouth extended, a cone shell crawls across another mollusc on the seabed. If the cone detects a fish, it fires its toxic harpoon out of its mouth.

CHEMICAL WEAPONS

IN NATURE, MANY ANIMALS USE POISONS TO WARD OFF THEIR ENEMIES, BUT VENOM IS PURPOSE-MADE TO KILL. The earliest chemical weapons evolved over a billion years ago, in micro-organisms that lived in water.
Since then, chemical techniques have also spread to life on land, but the world's most venomous animals still live in the sea. They include some deadly molluscs, such as cone shells, which inject their venom with tiny harpoons, and the world's most poisonous sea-snake, which bites fish with tiny, harmless-looking fangs. But the most toxic of these animals has no visible weapons at all. Instead, the box jellyfish injects its venom with a battery of specialised stinging cells, which explode within milliseconds of being touched.

Also known as the sea wasp, the box jellyfish gets its name from its rectangular body, or bell. It belongs to a family of animals called cubomedusas, which can be as small as a sugar cube. The box jellyfish is one of the biggest species, measuring up to 20 cm along each side, but because it is transparent, it is almost impossible to spot at sea. The adults are strong swimmers, and they steer towards daylight, guided by a cluster of small eyes at the corners of their bodies. From the Philippines all the way to northern Australia, box jellies make their way along coasts, trailing their deadly slender tentacles in the water below.

A box jellyfish's tentacles can be up to 3 m long, and they are covered with microscopic cells called cnidocytes. Each of these cells contains a tiny store of venom, and an inflatable

HANGING BY A THREAD A box jellyfish snags a banana prawn. After stinging the victim, the tentacles contract, reeling the prawn into the jellyfish's mouth.

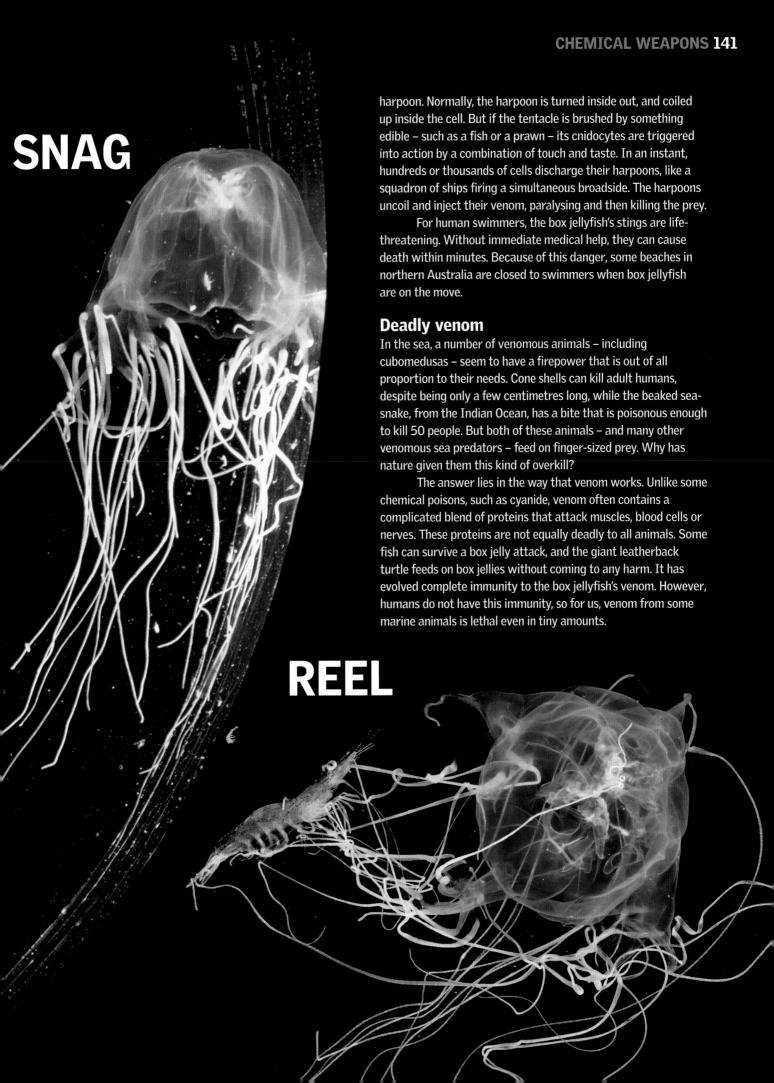

SNAG

harpoon. Normally, the harpoon is turned inside out, and coiled up inside the cell. But if the tentacle is brushed by something edible – such as a fish or a prawn – its cnidocytes are triggered into action by a combination of touch and taste. In an instant, hundreds or thousands of cells discharge their harpoons, like a squadron of ships firing a simultaneous broadside. The harpoons uncoil and inject their venom, paralysing and then killing the prey.

For human swimmers, the box jellyfish's stings are life-threatening. Without immediate medical help, they can cause death within minutes. Because of this danger, some beaches in northern Australia are closed to swimmers when box jellyfish are on the move.

Deadly venom

In the sea, a number of venomous animals – including cubomedusas – seem to have a firepower that is out of all proportion to their needs. Cone shells can kill adult humans, despite being only a few centimetres long, while the beaked sea-snake, from the Indian Ocean, has a bite that is poisonous enough to kill 50 people. But both of these animals – and many other venomous sea predators – feed on finger-sized prey. Why has nature given them this kind of overkill?

The answer lies in the way that venom works. Unlike some chemical poisons, such as cyanide, venom often contains a complicated blend of proteins that attack muscles, blood cells or nerves. These proteins are not equally deadly to all animals. Some fish can survive a box jelly attack, and the giant leatherback turtle feeds on box jellies without coming to any harm. It has evolved complete immunity to the box jellyfish's venom. However, humans do not have this immunity, so for us, venom from some marine animals is lethal even in tiny amounts.

REEL

Venomous animals on land

There are nearly 3000 kinds of snake, and they exert a mixture of fascination and repulsion, partly because of the way they move, but mainly because of the way they kill. Only about one in four snakes is actually venomous, but those that are include some of the most dangerous animals on land.

In terms of sheer killing power, the inland taipan or fierce snake tops the danger list. This Australian snake contains enough venom to kill about 100 people, or nearly quarter of a million mice. Despite its terrifying weaponry, it is a relatively timid creature and quickly flees if approached. As a result, it is responsible for very few human deaths. Far more dangerous are snakes with less potent venom, which strike back if they are caught by surprise. On average, for every ten of these species, one or two are especially dangerous, because they make a habit of hunting near buildings, or in farmland, or along the sides of forest paths.

In Central and South America, the terciopelo or fer-de-lance fits this description. A close relative of North America's rattlesnakes, it often hunts in fields and plantations, and is responsible for over 75 per cent of fatal snakebites in the American tropics – over 1000 deaths a year. The terciopelo attacks the instant that it is disturbed, and it has a dangerous tendency to leap as it strikes. Instead of being bitten on the feet, victims are often hit higher up the leg, reducing their chances of survival.

Africa's most dangerous snakes include the black mamba, which is reputed to be the world's fastest, with a top speed of over 20 km/h. But far more deaths are caused by the puff adder and gaboon viper, two large fat-bodied snakes that hunt by waiting for prey to come their way. Both are superbly camouflaged, and all too easy to step on as they lurk among fallen leaves. The gaboon viper's fangs are the longest of any snake – measuring up to 5 cm from base to tip – and this species also injects more venom than any other snake when it bites. The

largest number of snakebite fatalities, however, occur in southern Asia, with over 10 000 fatal attacks a year. Here, the main culprits are cobras and vipers – snakes that have an unnerving inclination to slither indoors in search of food.

Snake versus snake

Despite their deadly defences, even the world's most venomous snakes sometimes end up by being killed and eaten, particularly if they are not yet fully grown. Mongooses are famous for

attacking snakes, using their superior agility to bite them behind the head – a tactic that prevents most venomous snakes fighting back. And mongooses are not alone. In Africa, secretary birds often feed on snakes, while snake eagles attack them in many parts of the world, swooping down and gripping with their talons. But in the tropics, some of the most effective snake-eaters are snakes themselves.

The world's biggest venomous snake – the king cobra or hamadryad – feeds almost entirely on snakes, sometimes even its own species, tracking them down with its eyesight and superb sense of smell. Growing up to 5 m long, it lives deep in the snake-filled forests of South-east Asia. The king cobra is not immune to the venom of other snakes, but it has surprise on its size. Having bitten its victim, it begins to swallow it almost immediately – something that stops its prey biting back. Like most snakes, the cobra uses a side-to-side motion of its jaws to 'walk' its prey down its throat. With a long snake, the process can take several hours. By the time the cobra nears the tail, its victim's head is in its stomach, where digestion is already well underway.

SPRAY ATTACK Spitting cobras can fire their venom up to 3 m, from holes that open on the front of each fang. The venom can cause permanent blindness if it lands in the eyes.

CHEMICAL DEFENCES

BY USING TOXIC CHEMICALS, SMALL ANIMALS CAN FEND OFF ATTACKERS MANY TIMES THEIR OWN SIZE. Amphibians often use chemicals for self-defence, and so do many caterpillars – the merest brush with some of them can be enough to kill. While amphibians commonly spread their poisons over their skin to deter would-be predators, caterpillars have a different delivery system: their poisons are often stored inside ultra-fine hairs. In some caterpillars, the hairs are long and very visible, in others they are tiny, but very numerous. These hairs are often kept in small pockets along the caterpillar's sides. If the caterpillar is attacked, the pockets open, releasing clouds of hairs into the air.

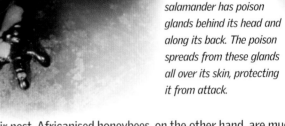

TOXIC SKIN The fire salamander has poison glands behind its head and along its back. The poison spreads from these glands all over its skin, protecting it from attack.

The caterpillars of pine processionary moths often use this kind of chemical defence. Their hairs have tips like microscopic harpoons, which quickly work their way into human skin. Once the hairs are embedded, they trigger a severe allergic rash. But even this is mild compared to the caterpillars of *Lonomia* moths, which live in the forests and open woodland of South America. The caterpillars are well camouflaged, which means that it is easy to touch them by mistake. When this happens, their hairs inject a powerful anticoagulant that can cause internal bleeding and kidney failure. In Brazil, this condition – called lonomiasis – causes several human deaths every year.

> The caterpillars of *Lonomia* moths in South American are well camouflaged, which means that it is easy to touch them by mistake. When this happens, their hairs inject a powerful anticoagulant that can cause internal bleeding and kidney failure.

Mass attacks

Caterpillars use chemical defences in a passive way. But social insects – which include bees and wasps – follow the well-known military principle that the best form of defence is a pre-emptive strike. Nearly all of these have venomous stings or bites, and because they live in giant family groups, their combined firepower can have an overwhelming effect. The amount of venom in a bee or wasp is typically about 0.5 mm^3 – about the same as in a droplet of light rain. But in a large nest, with tens of thousands of workers, the total venom reserve is easily enough to kill animals as big as a horse.

Fortunately, honeybees rarely stage mass attacks, and individuals seldom sting if not threatened, although they are quick to sting anything or anyone that tries to interfere with their nest. Africanised honeybees, on the other hand, are much more aggressive, and are much more likely to go on the offensive. Often known as 'killer bees', they are a hybrid form between European honeybees and African queen bees, which were accidentally released in Brazil in the late 1950s. Since then, they have spread northwards through South and Central America, reaching the southern states of the US. Here, they have caused over a dozen human deaths – a figure that looks likely to grow as the bees continue their advance.

Intruders on the loose

If chemical defences were 100 per cent foolproof, the world would soon be overrun by toxic animals. But just as with snake venom and jellyfish stings, not all wild animals are equally affected. In Africa, a mammal called the ratel breaks into bees' nests to get at their honey, and can be stung hundreds of times without being put off its food. In the air, bee-eaters have their own way of dealing with stings. They catch bees, and deactivate their stings by wiping them against a branch. Once that is done, the bee is swallowed whole. Stinging insects are also attacked by other insects, such as mites and cuckoo bees, which act as parasites in their nests.

But occasionally, a toxic animal finds itself with no enemies at all. This is what happened to the cane toad when it was brought from Central America to Australia in 1935. The cane toad was introduced to combat pests in sugar-cane plantations but it soon spread out of control. None of Australia's native predators could cope with its toxic skin, so the toad's chemical defence became the ultimate passport to success. Today, cane toads are found throughout northeast Australia where they are threatening important wildlife refuges, including Kakadu National Park.

PLANT POISONS

DURING THE 18TH CENTURY, THE UPAS TREE, FROM SOUTH-EAST ASIA, WAS BELIEVED TO GIVE OFF DEADLY FUMES. The story was an exaggeration (see box, right) but many plants do have lethal poisons which they use in self-defence. Among the most toxic plants are the strychnine tree, which grows in southern Asia, and deadly nightshade, a widespread plant in the northern hemisphere. Poison hemlock contains a deadly nerve-blocking agent called coniine, while the seeds of the castor-oil plant contain ricin – the most potent plant poison of all. Ricin has a toxicity higher than cobra venom: just one gram would be enough to kill 5000 people.

Plants contain thousands of chemicals, and many of their poisons started life as accidental by-products of the way that plants work. Over millions of years, evolution has slowly stepped up their production, because being poisonous is an excellent way of keeping animals at bay.

DEADLY ALLURE With their glossy skin and dark colour, deadly nightshade berries look good enough to eat. Many birds feed on them without coming to any harm, but just four or five are enough to kill an adult human. The entire plant is highly poisonous.

HEALTH HAZARD Giant hogweed is one of the world's tallest perennial plants, growing up from ground level each spring. The whole of the plant produces phototoxic sap, but the worst injuries come from handling its bristly stems.

Killer stinging nettles

Most plant poisons take effect only when they are swallowed. Many of them have a bitter taste, which in the wild works in a plant's favour by warning animals to leave it alone. But with some plants, the poison doesn't even have to be swallowed. Just touching the plant is enough to trigger a reaction.

In many parts of the world, the common nettle is a well-known stinging plant. When brushed, its bristles release formic acid – the same poison that is used by stinging ants. Stings from common nettles can be painful, but in New Zealand, the ongaonga, or nettle tree, has far worse effects than this. Growing up to 3 m tall, this straggling bush bristles with stiff stinging hairs that pack a tremendous punch. This plant has been known to kill dogs, cattle and horses, and has caused at least one human death in New Zealand's recent history.

Lingering poison

Poison ivy, from North America, is probably the most famous of the 'untouchables' of the plant world. A climber that grows in woods and along riverbanks, it looks quite harmless, with shiny leaves divided into three parts and small creamy yellow flowers. But appearances are deceptive. The entire plant is covered with urushiol – a sticky oil that produces a violent allergic reaction if it comes into contact with human skin. Unlike plant sap, urushiol chemically binds to skin, so once it has been in place for a few minutes, it cannot be washed off.

In most people, the effects begin within minutes, but it takes a day or two for the worst symptoms to get underway. The skin breaks out in a bright red rash and starts to swell. These swellings become more and more itchy, forming watery blisters that eventually burst. It is a painful and long-lasting experience, and the rash can take up to three weeks to subside. Urushiol often gets on clothes, where it can stay active for months or even years. And if poison ivy is burned, tiny droplets of urushiol are carried away in smoke, which if inhaled – even far downwind – can trigger off a potentially fatal reaction.

Pernicious giant

During the 19th century, the owners of Britain's country houses were avid collectors of new plants brought back from far-flung parts of the world. One of the most imposing was giant hogweed – a statuesque perennial from the Caucasus Mountains, on the dividing line between Europe and Asia. Giant hogweed can grow to 5 m high and bears huge white flowerheads. For gardeners in search of instant impact, it seemed like the perfect plant.

Unfortunately, it is also poisonous – in a highly unusual way. Hogweed stems and leaves produce a watery sap, which is harmless in subdued light. But in bright sunlight it undergoes a chemical change, triggering a rash even worse than the one caused by poison ivy, often leaving permanent scars. Before the danger was widely recognised, giant hogweed was already a popular garden plant throughout northern Europe, and in parts of North America. To make matters worse, it escaped into the wild and today this giant has taken a firm hold in both continents.

MIXED BLESSING The opium poppy is the source of morphine – a highly effective painkiller, but also a dangerously addictive drug.

A SINISTER REPUTATION

For centuries, milky sap from the upas tree was used to make poison arrows by hunters in Indonesia. The poison is a cardiac glycoside – a substance that works by stopping the heart. In 1783, a Dutch surgeon, N. P. Foersch, wrote a report about the tree, and decided to add some imaginative details of his own. He claimed that the tree gave off deadly fumes, which could kill all living things in a radius of up to 25 km. The report was believed by European naturalists, and for decades, the upas tree was thought to be the deadliest plant in the world.

CAMOUFLAGE

BLENDING IN WITH THE BACKGROUND IS A CLASSIC WAY OF OUTWITTING YOUR ENEMIES. On land, camouflage is used by some large predators, such as pythons, tigers and polar bears. But the most effective camouflage belongs to much smaller animals, such as insects. These creatures are all easily visible when they move, but as soon as they stop they seem to disappear. It's the perfect way to avoid being eaten – or to catch even smaller animal prey unawares.

Disappearing tricks

There are nearly 30 major groups of insects, and almost all of them contain animals that use camouflage at some stage of their lives. But a handful have developed camouflage to an incredible degree. Leaders of the field are the stick and leaf insects – slow-moving vegetarians that need constant protection from predatory birds.

Stick insects have the most stretched-out bodies in the insect world. Many are over 6 cm long, but the biggest species, from the forests of Borneo, measure up to 50 cm. Thanks to their stick-like shape and colour, all of them are invisible when they feed in bushes and trees. Leaf insects are just as impressive, but their bodies are flat, with spreading wings. Complete with tiny blemishes, and ribs that look like veins, they are amazingly effective imitators of leaves, even down to details such as swaying gently in the breeze.

Because leaves are everywhere in nature, tens of thousands of insects use leaf-like shapes and colours in their camouflage. There are also leaf-like fish, leaf-like spiders and even leaf-like frogs and toads. Tiny leaf chameleons from Madagascar are some of the world's smallest reptiles, measuring just 3 cm long. At this size, there is little point in fighting back against snakes or birds. Instead, blending in with the background is the best strategy for survival.

LEAF MIMIC Like many camouflaged animals, this caterpillar has markings that break up the outline of its body.

WAITING FOR TAKE OFF Until its newly formed wings have hardened, this black-tailed skimmer dragonfly protects itself from insect-eating birds by hiding in tall grass, its upright body blending in with its surroundings.

HIDDEN GATHERING (overleaf) Australian leaf-tailed geckos are perfectly camouflaged on fallen leaves or against the bark of trees. How many can you spot?

NO HIDING PLACE

PLANTS MAKE A PERFECT BACKDROP FOR CAMOUFLAGED ANIMALS, BECAUSE THERE IS SO MUCH TO HIDE AGAINST. BUT EVEN OUT IN THE OPEN, CAMOUFLAGE CAN HELP ANIMALS TO STAY CONCEALED. Few land habitats provide less cover than deserts, with their wide open vistas and razor-sharp skylines. But even when they look empty, they are often home to hidden animals. One of the best ways to find these animals is to go for a walk. Suddenly, the ground comes to life. Grasshoppers leap into the air to avoid being trodden on, while lizards scuttle across the ground. These animals only give themselves away when they move.

FACTS

THE CHAMELEON PRAWN
CHANGES COLOUR TO BLEND IN WITH its background. During the day, it matches brown, red or green seaweeds, or even the mottled colour of seabed sand. At night, its colour changes to greyish blue.

THE GRAMA GRASS cactus has long ribbon-like spines that look like the leaves of dead grass. It uses its camouflage to hide from animals looking for water and food.

THE X-RAY FISH
GETS ITS NAME FROM ITS see-through body. Its muscles are almost transparent, and the rest of its internal organs are hidden inside a silvery pouch.

FACTS

Despite their name, grasshoppers rarely eat grass. In deserts, most of them feed on drought-resistant shrubs, and seeds scattered by the wind. For protection, they often look exactly like pebbles, with round stippled bodies, and even camouflaged streaks across their eyes. Their camouflage can change each time they moult or shed their skins. Young desert grasshoppers often resemble small pieces of quartz, while the adults blend in with broken rock or sand. It is a superb self-defence, until something threatening comes really close.

Faced with danger, most desert grasshoppers wait until the last minute and then suddenly launch themselves into the air. At this point, their camouflage vanishes, and they reveal brilliantly coloured hind wings. This 'flash coloration' is part of the escape strategy: it startles predators and throws them even more off course when the grasshopper lands, and the vivid colours suddenly disappear.

Living stones

Very few plants use camouflage, but deserts are the habitat of most of those that do. The best disguises belong to thimble-sized succulents called living stones, which come from the deserts of southern Africa. There are about 40 species of living stones, and all of them have a pair of flat-topped fleshy leaves. Like desert grasshoppers, their leaves have mottled markings that look like patterns in rock, which is how they get their name.

For most of the year, living stones are almost impossible to see, because they blend in so well with their surroundings. The first European botanist to identify them only realised that they were plants, rather than stones, when he discovered they had roots. But once a year – typically in late winter – living stones burst into flower. For a few weeks they abandon their camouflage and put on a bright show to attract insect visitors.

See-through animals

If deserts are difficult places for camouflage, the open sea is even harder. Near the surface, there is no cover of any kind, putting creatures at risk from seabirds flying overhead, and from all kinds of predators swimming deeper down. Faced with this double danger, many small animals use the ultimate disguise: their bodies are completely see-through.

Transparency is rare in vertebrates because their bodies contain cartilage or bone. But in the sea, huge numbers of invertebrates let light shine straight through. Most jellyfish have a milky hue, but animals called salps are often as transparent as glass. Measuring a few millimetres long, they are among the most abundant animals in the seas. Ctenophores, or sea gooseberries, are almost as common. They are invisible by day, but at night they shimmer with green light if disturbed. This eerie display can continue for many minutes, until the light fades, and the sea turns black once more.

STONE PLANTS Living stones have two leaves, separated by a cleft that conceals the stem. Despite their small size, they can live for many years.

PREVIOUS PAGE There are three geckos.

DECORATOR CRAB

THE ELEGANT DECORATOR CRAB IS AN
EXPERT IN THE ART OF SELF-DISGUISE. INSTEAD OF USING SPEED TO
ESCAPE FROM DANGER, IT MAKES A PERSONAL JACKET OF LIVING
CAMOUFLAGE. Clambering over the seabed, the crab – one of many decorator crabs
living in shallow water near coasts, or on coral reefs – picks up small animals and
pieces of seaweed in its claws, and then carefully fastens them to its body case. Once
they are in place, they start to grow, breaking up
the crab's outline, so that it becomes almost
impossible to see until it starts to move. As well
as collecting living things, the crab also gathers
pieces of debris, such as wood chips and
fragments of shell. All of this is kept in place by
hundreds of tiny hooks which are scattered over
the crab's legs and carapace, or shell.

Every few months, the elegant decorator
crab has to shed its body case – along with its
camouflage – so that it can grow again. Rather
than rebuilding the camouflage from scratch,
the crab carefully removes the plants and animals from the old case and fastens them
onto the new one. This natural recycling means that many of the plants and animals
that it carries stay aboard throughout the crab's life.

CLASS: Malacostraca

ORDER: Decapoda

SPECIES: *Oregonia gracilis*

HABITAT: Sandy and rocky shores

DISTRIBUTION: Pacific coast of
Canada and USA

KEY FEATURES: Camouflages itself
by attaching living animals and
small pieces of seaweed to its
body case

MIMICRY

INSTEAD OF BLENDING INTO THEIR BACKGROUND, MIMICS SET OUT TO BE SEEN. These actors of the animal world include caterpillars that impersonate snakes and crocodiles that look like branches drifting downstream. Mimics copy all kinds of objects, but the most gifted ones copy other animals. They don't simply look like the animals they are copying – they often behave like them, too, and in some cases even smell like them. Almost all do it for the same reason: to make themselves look more dangerous than they really are.

Mimicry is very rare among large animals, such as mammals and birds. Being a tiger mimic, for example, would be too complex to be worthwhile. But with much smaller animals, impostors are everywhere. Many of these mimics imitate bees and wasps, but the accolade for the 'most-copied animal' is easily won by ants. Ants live on almost every land habitat on Earth, and predators that try to eat them soon learn that they fight back furiously if attacked. As a result, looking like an ant can be a passport to survival success.

The list of ant mimics includes an amazing collection of different insects, such as flies, bugs, beetles and even young praying mantises. But the most talented ant mimics are spiders, which have evolved stretched-out bodies with dark markings and a narrow

If they are spotted by a predator, some camouflaged caterpillars turn to mimicry as a last resort. Hunching up the front of their bodies, they display two staring spots of colour that look like eyes. The effect is pure theatre: in an instant, the caterpillar seems to transform itself into a snake.

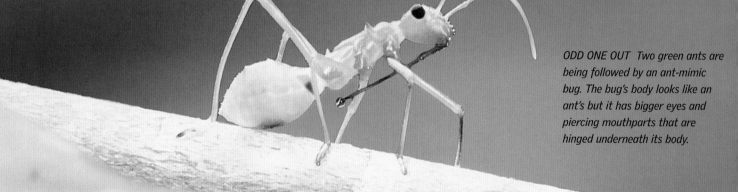

ODD ONE OUT Two green ants are being followed by an ant-mimic bug. The bug's body looks like an ant's but it has bigger eyes and piercing mouthparts that are hinged underneath its body.

COSTUME CHANGE This young tiger swallowtail caterpillar is disguised as a bird dropping. When it gets bigger this mimicry no longer works, so it turns green to hide among leaves.

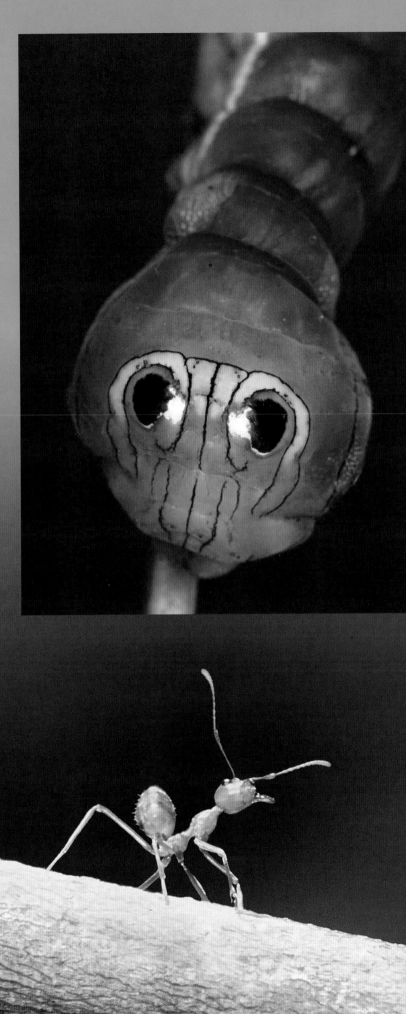

SNAKE IMITATOR With its staring eyespots, this caterpillar from Costa Rica looks like a miniature snake.

ant-like 'waist'. Spiders have eight legs, while ants have only six. To get around this anatomical problem, ant-mimic spiders often hold their front legs in the air, so they look like an ant's feelers or antennae. To complete the illusion, they have the same jerky movements as ants, and they keep on the move in a very unspiderlike way. Some of them run alongside real ants, and a few even prey on the ants they copy, without the ants realising that they have a stranger in their midst.

Grand illusions

Caterpillars are the sitting ducks of the insect world. Slow-moving and thin-skinned, they usually eat out in the open, which makes them easy targets for birds. Some are protected by poisonous chemicals or hairs, but huge numbers of them depend on camouflage or mimicry to survive.

Camouflaged caterpillars are often superbly disguised, but if they are spotted by a predator, some turn to mimicry as a last resort. Hunching up the front of their bodies, they display two staring spots of colour that look like eyes. The effect is pure theatre: in an instant, the caterpillar seems to transform itself into a snake. To human eyes, its tiny size gives the game away, but the trickery is often enough to frighten birds. Once the bird has gone, the caterpillar resumes its normal shape.

EMERGENCY ESCAPES

IN NATURE, EVEN THE BEST DEFENCES CAN FAIL, AND ANIMALS CAN ALSO GET ACCIDENTALLY TRAPPED. For many, it spells the end, but some use extreme measures to escape. One of the most drastic is autotomy – literally 'self-amputation'.

The human body does not contain any parts that can be easily shed, so for us, autotomy is a highly risky business. In 2003, a young climber in Utah found this out for himself, when a giant boulder rolled down a slope, trapping one of his arms. After five days waiting for help, he eventually cut through his arm with a penknife, a drastic action that saved his life. For certain animals, autotomy can also be life-saving, but it is not something that needs any equipment at all. Instead, body parts break off along special lines of weakness, allowing their owners to make an emergency escape. In many cases, the missing parts are then slowly replaced.

Sacrificial tails

Lizards are particularly good at this radical escape trick, and they do it by shedding their tails. If a lizard is caught by a predator, special muscles contract near the tail's base, breaking it off at its weakest point. The tail drops off and wriggles energetically for several minutes, distracting the predator while the lizard makes its getaway. During this operation, the lizard loses very little blood, and the stump quickly heals. Over the following months, a new tail gradually grows in its place. This new tail often has a different pattern of scales, and contains cartilage instead of bone. However, it functions just as well as the old one, and if danger strikes again, it can be shed in turn.

Some lizards make this defence even more effective by having brightly coloured tails, or by waving their tails above their backs. But every time a lizard loses its tail, it also loses the nutrients that were needed to grow it. It's a problem that some lizards solve in an extraordinary way. Once the danger has passed, the lizard returns to the scene and searches for the tail that it has shed

If a lizard is caught by a predator, special muscles contract near the tail's base, breaking it off at its weakest point. The tail drops off and wriggles energetically for several minutes, distracting the predator while the lizard makes its getaway.

If it finds it, it swallows the tail whole. This self-cannibalism may not sound very appealing, but it allows the lizard to recycle nutrients that would otherwise have gone to waste.

Shedding arms and legs

In emergencies, insects, spiders and harvestmen often abandon one or more of their legs. These usually break off close to their bodies, although in harvestmen, the break occurs further down the leg itself. Tarantulas can regrow missing legs at any time during their lives, but for most adult insects and spiders, a lost leg is gone for good. However, as they have lots of legs to start with, this is not such a handicap as it sounds. Harvestmen can survive with just four of their eight legs, while most beetles can make do with four. Adult grasshoppers are very prone to losing back legs, but they can hop almost as far with a single back leg as they can with two.

In the sea, crabs and lobsters can regrow missing legs and missing claws at any stage of their lives – a big advantage for animals that are often nipped and bitten by fish. However, starfish outshine most other sea animals at replacing missing parts. Lost arms slowly grow back, provided that the central part of the starfish's body is intact. In some starfish, lost arms can turn into complete new starfish. However, it is a slow process, taking months or even years to produce a starfish with symmetrical arms.

EXPLOSIVE AFTERMATH A leopard sea cucumber lies covered in defensive threads, after fending off an attacker. The threads are sticky but the sea cucumber shrugs them off when it moves.

Self-evisceration

Sea cucumbers are relatives of starfish, but their sausage-shaped bodies have no arms to lose. Instead, these slow-moving inhabitants of the seabed have a particularly bizarre form of emergency defence. If a sea cucumber is threatened, it turns its anus towards its adversary and takes careful aim. It then builds up pressure inside its body, and squirts out a cluster of sticky threads that look like strands of fine spaghetti. These threads are attached to the sea cucumber's breathing system, but they break off as they burst out into the water. If the aim is good, its enemy becomes entangled in a gluey mass and the sea cucumber crawls away. Over a period of weeks, sea cucumbers can replace the threads that they have fired.

Periodically, sea cucumbers expel not just threads, but almost all of their internal organs as well. This sometimes happens when they feel threatened, but in many species, it takes place at particular times of year. For these animals, self-evisceration seems to be a normal way of getting rid of waste – one of the most extreme forms of 'routine housekeeping' in the animal world.

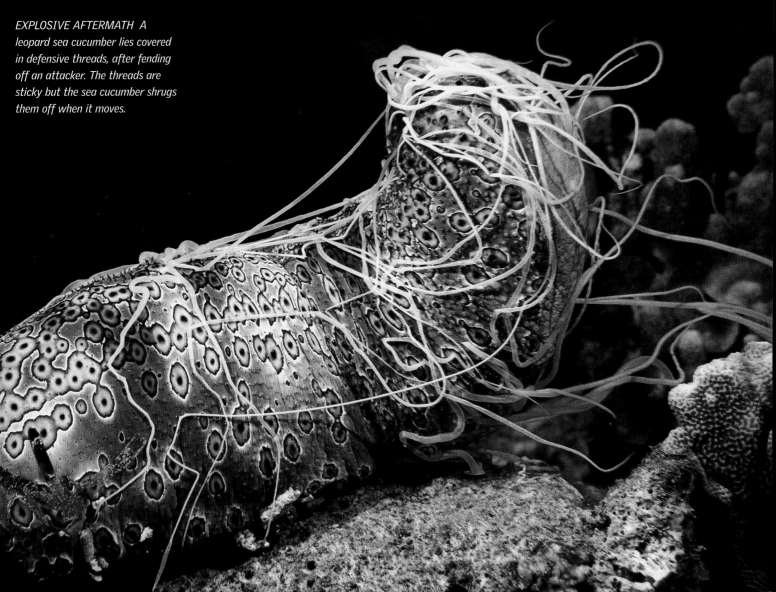

INDEX

PICTURE CREDITS

Abbreviations:
T = top; M = middle; B = bottom;
L = left; R = right

Front cover: FLPA/Minden Pictures/ZSSD
Back cover: naturepl.com/ARCO/Lucasseck **1** National Geographic Image Collection/Klaus Nigge. **2-7** B & C Alexander/Arcticphoto.com. **3** photolibrary.com/Oxford Scientific, TL; Still Pictures/Francois Gilson, TR; FLPA/Minden Pictures/Michael & Patricia Fogden, ML. **4** naturepl.com/Bruce Davidson, ML; photolibrary.com/Alan & Sandy Carey, BM. **5** photolibrary.com/Animals Animals/Earth Scenes, TL; photolibrary.com/OSF/Robert Tyrell, MR; ardea.com/Brian Bevan, BL; FLPA/David Hosking, BR. **5-6** Getty Images/Graeme Robertson. **6** National Geographic Image Collection/Steve Winter, ML; photolibrary.com (Australia)/Rob Blakers, BL; Science Photo Library/John Walsh, R; Natural History Museum, London, BR. **3-6** FLPA/Minden Pictures/Ingo Arndt (background). **8-9** FLPA/Minden Pictures/Norbert Wu. **10-11** left to right: naturepl.com/Gary K. Smith, 1; National Geographic Image Collection/Beverley Joubert, 2; NHPA/J. & A. Scott, 3; Science Photo Library/ Sinclair Stammers, 4; Auscape/D. Parer & E. Parer-Cook, 5; photolibrary.com, 6; National Geographic Image Collection/Jozsef Szentpeteri, 7. **12-13** left to right: National Geographic Image Collection/George Grall, 1; FLPA/Jurgen & Christine Sohns, 2; Science Photo Library/Dr John Brackenbury, 3; NHPA/Nigel J. Dennis, 4; SeaPics.com/Gary Bell, 5; Still Pictures/Geoffrey Stewart, 6; photolibrary.com/ Pacific Stock (background). **14-15** Minden Pictures/Mitsuaki Iwago. **16-17** photolibrary.com/ Imagestate Ltd/L.Peck Michael. **16** naturepl.com/ ARCO/Lucasseck, MR; ardea.com/Ferrero-Labat, BR. **18-19** NHPA/Nigel J. Dennis. **20** naturepl.com/Gary K. Smith. **21** Corbis/Charles Krebs. **22** ardea.com/ John Daniels. **23** ardea.com/N. N. Birks. **24-25** DRK Photo/S. Nielson. **24** Hedgehog Houze NZ/Jason Elsworth, B. **25** aviation-images.com/K.Tokunaga, TR; Mountain Camera Picture Library/John Cleare, MR. **26-27** National Geographic Image Collection/ Jozsef Szentpeteri. **27** naturepl.com/David Kjaer. **28-29** SeaPics.com/Avi Klapfer. **28** photolibrary.com/ Richard Herrmann. **29** SeaPics.com/Robin W. Baird, T. **30** Irina Lynch. **31** photolibrary.com/Mark Stouffer, L; photolibrary.com/David Fleetham, R. **32** photolibrary.com/Ben Osborne. **33** SeaPics.com/ Steve Drogin, TL, TR; SeaPics.com/Howard Hall 2004, B. **34-35** naturepl.com/Jose B. Ruiz. **34** naturepl.com/Jose B. Ruiz, TL; SeaPics.com/Yoshi Hirata, BR. **35** DRK Photo/Michael Fogden, TR; naturepl.com/Jose B. Ruiz, BR. **36-37** National Geographic Image Collection/Beverley Joubert. **38-39** Corbis/Michael T. Sedam. **38** photolibrary.com/Charles Lindsay. **40** National Geographic Image Collection/Kim Wolhuter. **41** DRK Photo/Fritz Poelking. **42** FLPA/Foto Natura/Flip de Nooyer. **43** National Geographic Image Collection/Annie Griffiths Belt. **44** Reuters/Gleb Garanich. **45** photolibrary.com. **46-47** Science Photo Library/Leonard Rue Enterprises. **47** National Geographic Image Collection/Maria Stenzel, T; naturepl.com/Cindy Buxton, M. **48** Science Photo Library/James King-Holmes, T; Alamy/blickwinkel, B. **49** National Geographic Image Collection/James L. Stanfield, B. **50** SeaPics.com. **51** Dr Dennis Cullinane. **52-53** FLPA/Minden Pictures/Flip Nicklin. **54** (c) Merlin Tuttle Bat Conservation International, T; ardea.com/Bob Gibbons, B. **55** naturepl.com/ David Welling, L; photolibrary.com/OSF/Robert Tyrell, R. **56-57** SeaPics.com/Duncan Murrell. **58** photolibrary.com, BL. **58-59** FLPA/Ariadne Van Zandbergen. **59** NHPA/J. & A. Scott. **60** NHPA/Daniel Heuclin. **61** ardea.com/Chris Harvey. **62-63** DRK Photo/Fritz Poelking. **63** NHPA/Andrew Bailey, T. **64-65** photolibrary.com. **65** DRK Photo/Norbert Wu, T. **66** photolibrary.com (Australia)/Ted Mead. **67** National Geographic Image Collection/Jonathan Blair. **68-69** DRK Photo/Thomas Dressler. **69** Auscape/Frank Woerle,

TR. **70-71** Science Photo Library/John Walsh. **72** FLPA/Minden Pictures/Gerry Ellis. **73** Still Pictures/Gary Gaugler, TR; Science Photo Library/Juergen Berger, ML; Still Pictures/Geoffrey Stewart, BM. **74** FLPA/Minden Pictures/Flip Nicklin. **75** Science Photo Library/Eye of Science, T; Still Pictures/Volker Steger, B. **76** (c) 2003 Ana Signorovitch, ML; Science Photo Library/Andrew Syred, BR. **77** Science Photo Library/Sinclair Stammers. **78** National Geographic Image Collection/George Grall. **79** Science Photo Library/David Aubrey, TL; Science Photo Library/Dr John Brackenbury, R. **80** Still Pictures/J. Meul. **81** Shutterstock/Phil Morley. **82** NHPA/Michael Leach. **82-83** naturepl.com/Kim Taylor. **84-85** photolibrary.com/Pacific Stock/Greg Vaughn. **86** NHPA/Andy Rouse, L. **86-87** DRK Photo 1996/M. C. Chamberlain. **87** Auscape/Fritz Polking, TR; ML; Auscape John Canalosi, MR. **88** DRK Photo/Stanley Breeden. **89** naturepl.com/ARCO/Lucasseck. **90** SeaPics.com/Jeff Rotman. **91** DRK Photo/Martin Harvey, T; Still Pictures/F. Hecker, B. **92-93** FLPA/Larry West. **94** DRK Photo/Fritz Polking, T; DRK Photo/David Falconer, B. **94-95** photolibrary.com. **95** naturepl.com/Ingo Arndt, R. **96** Auscape/Densey Clyne, TL; Auscape/D. Parer & E. Parer-Cook, BL. **97** Alamy/Rosemary Calvert, TL; FLPA/Minden Pictures/Michael & Patricia Fogden, B. **98** NHPA/Kevin Schafer. **99** FLPA/Jurgen & Christine Sohns. **100** naturepl.com/ARCO/Meul. **101** Auscape/PHO.N.E/Pascal Goetgheluck. **102** National Geographic Image Collection/Jason Edwards. **103** National Geographic Image Collection/Tim Laman. **104-105** FLPA/Ariadne Van Zandbergen. **106-107** SeaPics.com/Gary Bell. **108** NHPA/Daniel Heuclin, T; National Geographic Image Collection/George Grall, BL. **109** DRK Photo/Michael Fogden. **110-111** SeaPics.com/ Stephen Wong. **112** National Geographic Image Collection/Brian J. Skerry. **112-113** ardea.com/Paul Van Gaalen, T. **113** photolibrary.com/ Phototake.Inc/Dennis Kunkel, B. **114** Science Photo Library/Martin Dohrn. **115** DRK Photo/Don Pat Valenti, BM; Roy Williams, BL; BR. **116** photolibrary.com/Owen Newman. **117** naturepl.com/Michael Durham. **118** ardea.com/Ken Lucas. **119** FLPA/Minden Pictures/Norbert Wu. **120** Andrew Brown. **121** naturepl.com/Jeff Rotman, L; FLPA/B. Borrell Casals, R. **122** naturepl.com /Simon Wagen/J. Downer Product, L; DRK Photo/Marty Cordano, R. **123** FLPA/Albert Visage. **124** naturalvisions.co.uk/Simon Brown. **124-125** Science Photo Library/Hermann Eisenbeiss. **126-127** naturepl.com/Karl Ammann. **128** naturepl.com/Kim Taylor. **129** naturepl.com/John Downer. **130-131** photolibrary.com/Rex Butcher. **131** NHPA/Photoshot/Stephen Krasemann. **132-133** National Geographic Image Collection/George Grall. **134** David Doubilet. **135** naturepl.com/Staffan Widstrand. **136** National Geographic Image Collection/Joel Sartore. **137** FLPA/Sunset. **138** photolibrary.com. **139** FLPA/Foto Natura/Hans Leijense. **140** naturepl.com/Jeff Rotman, TL; NHPA/Peter Parks, TR. **140-141** National Geographic Image Collection/David Doubilet. **141** National Geographic Image Collection/David Doubilet, BR. **142** naturepl.com/John Downer/ Michael Richards. **143** naturalvisions.co.uk/ Francesco Tomasinelli. **144** FLPA/Bob Gibbons, TL; FLPA/Roger Wilmshurst, BR. **145** naturepl.com/ Jose B. Ruiz. **146** National Geographic Image Collection/George Grall, TR. **146-147** National Geographic Image Collection/Josef Szentpeteri. **148-149** National Geographic Image Collection/George Grall. **150** FLPA/Peggy Heard. **151** Brandon Cole/brandoncole.com. **152-153** naturepl.com/Mark Taylor. 152 National Geographic Image Collection/Robert Sisson, BL. **153** FLPA/Minden Pictures/Foto Natura/Ingo Arndt, TR. **154** Auscape/Greg Harold. **154-155** FLPA/Minden Pictures/Fred Bavendam.

Artworks:
Bradbury & Williams: pages 25; 27B; 51; 89;
Glyn Walton LINEDESIGN: pages 16, 47BR; 49TR;

NATURE'S MIGHTY POWERS: EXTREME NATURE
was published by The Reader's Digest Association Ltd, London. It was created and produced for Reader's Digest by Toucan Books Ltd, London.

The Reader's Digest Association Ltd,
11 Westferry Circus,
Canary Wharf,
London E14 4HE
www.readersdigest.co.uk

First edition copyright © 2008

Written by
David Burnie and David Helton

FOR TOUCAN BOOKS
Editors Jane Chapman, Andrew Kerr-Jarrett
Picture researchers Mia Stewart-Wilson, Christine Vincent, Caroline Wood
Proofreader Marion Dent
Indexer Michael Dent
Design Bradbury and Williams

FOR READER'S DIGEST
Project editor Christine Noble
Art editor Julie Bennett
Pre-press account manager Penny Grose
Product production manager Claudette Bramble
Production controller Katherine Bunn

READER'S DIGEST, GENERAL BOOKS
Editorial director Julian Browne
Art director Anne-Marie Bulat

Colour origination Colour Systems Ltd, London
Printed and bound in China

We are committed to both the quality of our products and the service we provide to our customers. We value your comments, so please feel free to contact us on 08705 113366 or via our website at **www.readersdigest.co.uk**

If you have any comments or suggestions about the content of our books, you can email us at **gbeditorial@readersdigest.co.uk**

CONCEPT CODE: UK0138/G/S
BOOK CODE: 636-004 UP0000-1
ISBN: 978-0-276-44292-6
ORACLE CODE: 356500015H.00.24